Invisible assets
FE in the educational market-place

by
Ernest Theodossin

ISBN: 0-907659-76-4

Published by The Staff College
Coombe Lodge
Blagdon
Bristol
BS18 6RG

Contents

Acknowledgements

The quantitative analysis of these materials has been carried out in the summer of 1990 by three stalwart assistants - Alan Finlayson, Monica Gomez and Anita Vettier - for whose help I am grateful, although I alone am responsible for the qualitative analysis. I would also like to record my thanks to Margaret King and colleagues at The Staff College library for continuing good-natured assistance with difficult requests.

List of tables

Chapter 1:
Cinderella and the invisible man

The somewhat oblique genesis of this study was a talk by the then Secretary of State for Education and Science, Kenneth Baker, to the Association of Colleges for Further and Higher Education (ACFHE) in February 1989. Getting a high-profile senior minister to address staff in the further education (FE) service counts as a special event, and Mr Baker used the occasion to put across a dramatic, if unexpected, message. He suggested to a gathering of senior college managers that FE is referred to by some as 'the Cinderella of the education service', adding for good measure that FE has 'a dowdy image' and 'what is undeniably a low profile' (Baker, 1989).

None of this could have startled those who work in and know FE, but by stating it publicly Mr Baker put the FE 'image problem' on the visible education agenda. The minister then called for 'an initiative to promote further education', challenging FE to set itself the goal of attracting 'more people into your colleges by selling yourselves even better'.

The Baker 'Cinderella' speech was delivered more than two years ago and is (almost ancient) education history. Its author is no longer at the Department of Education and Science (DES). Two Cabinet reshuffles in quick succession have yielded two other education ministers, and the present incumbent, Kenneth Clarke, has produced an FE White Paper (DES, 1991) that is in some respects even more exceptional than the Baker speech: FE is seldom enough the focus of ministerial reflection, but even less often the object of government action.

It would be agreeable to think that the White Paper was FE's long-owed national recognition, a coming of age, Cinderella moving into the palace. Not quite. The impulse behind the Paper owes as much to political expediency as to educational vision: the need to tackle an unpopular Community Charge. As a Times Educational Supplement article (Jackson,1991a) suggests, the initial March 1991 decision to take colleges out of LEA control

...showed every sign of being hurried out for political reasons – further education accounts for more than £2 billion of local government's spending...[The announcement] left huge gaps to be filled in by a White Paper promised in a couple of months' time.

It has since become apparent that the May 1991 White Paper was as rushed as the actual decision. The Paper's 107 pages are generously spread among two volumes, printed with nearly three-inch margins, and include 14 blank sides and 29 whole pages given over to chapter titles (at 18 per cent of the total surely a record), with the same three photographs (of specimen students) printed 21 times. The Paper's recommendations aim to revolutionise the organisation and funding of FE by bringing incorporation to the colleges and removing them from local education authority (LEA) control, but much remains to be worked out: funding arrangements; the role of Training and Enterprise Councils (TECs); the place of adult education and the careers service; training credits (endorsed before the pilot studies have been completed); etc.

There are exhortations on the need to eradicate the academic-vocational class divide, but few hints about how the necessary cultural revolution is to be achieved. More general National Vocational Qualifications (NVQs) are to be produced, and they are being worked on while I write. A system of Advanced and Ordinary Diplomas is promised 'at the earliest practicable date'.

On the positive side, the Paper has brought FE out of the wings and on to the education stage, even if not yet downstage centre. Nor are altered funding arrangements and a new legal status in a public sector providing agency likely in themselves to metamorphose popular images and public stereotypes. The Baker epithet persists: Cinderella still awaits rescue. Whatever else it may or may not be, the White Paper is not in itself an 'initiative to promote further education'. For that, much more is required, and, as I shall argue, it needs to come not from politicians from those who work in FE.

To the outsider, education may appear static, but underneath change is stirring, even if more perceptibly in some places than in others. If there is not yet an FE initiative, grand and all-embracing, there are at least several modest efforts in progress (identified in later pages) and – perhaps the most important legacies of Mr Baker's talk – a growing acceptance that FE has an image problem, and an emerging recognition that only FE can change its image and resolve the problem.

Big numbers and low visibility

In one of GK Chesterton's (1954) Father Brown stories, the murder mystery which has defeated less astute minds is at last solved by the cunning cleric: an invisible man must have committed the crime, someone

> ...dressed rather handsomely in red, blue and gold...and [who] in this striking, and even showy, costume... entered Himaylaya Mansions under eight human eyes: he killed Smythe in cold blood... came down into the street again carrying the dead body in his arms...
> ...and was never seen.

The culprit, of course, is the postman – or The Invisible Man, as the title has it – someone whose existence is known about by virtually everyone and who is regularly observed by hundreds of people without actually being noticed. Except for their being anything but showy, FE colleges can be viewed as education's equivalent – local, present, approachable and operating in full glare, but somehow easily ignored.

Although most of us would feel deprived if we had to do without postmen (or women) for any length of time, we tend to undervalue them. They are seldom treated seriously, as we might as a matter of course treat our bank manager or solicitor, neither of whom we see as often and neither of whom impacts so regularly on our daily lives. The postman is a servant, a facilitating transition between writer and recipient, a means to an end and hence interchangeable: one will do as well as another. He covers a large territory and serves people briefly. And so on... The analogy with FE colleges is easily sustained.

Low visibility is Cinders' problem as well. Like the postman, she is a servant and, as such, meant to perform effectively without impinging on anyone's consciousness. Confined to domestic drudgery, she can expect to remain unnoticed. Without a Fairy Godparent, Cinderella's future is joyless, and it is this image which usually attaches to the pejorative use of her name. For an activity or a person to be labelled or treated as a Cinderella is to be regarded as inconsequential.

Like so many females socialised into stereotyped roleplaying, Cinderella is desperately in need of assertiveness training. When she is finally rescued, it is through the determination of her Prince Charming and in spite of all the obstacles put in her way by her scheming stepfamily: Cinders has done absolutely nothing to help the good or thwart the wicked. She seems incapable of appreciating that drudges are made, not born, and they remain victims because they connive with and support their own bondage.

Why then should anyone – least of all a minister of state – link Cinderella with the FE service? Do Cinders' inertia, weakness and ineffectiveness truly parallel FE's own nature? In the house of education, is FE no more than an irrelevant, ignored and downtrodden servant?

If so, none of the statistical facts about FE colleges explains such relatively humble status. FE is defined (Hall, 1990) as

> ...those courses at (or below) the level of the General Certificate of Education (GCE) Advanced level or the Scottish Certificate of Education (SCE) Higher grade, or the Business and Technician [now Technology] Education Council (BTEC) National awards or the Scottish Vocational Education Council (SCOTVEC) awards.

Since colleges of further education (CFEs) are also usually taken to include adult education (AE), millions of people study in FE colleges each year.

Table 1 gives an overview of all United Kingdom (UK) home pupils and students in 1987-88[1] and **Table 2** provides comparable statistics for students aged 16+. **Table 3** shows the percentage of the young home population engaged in education from the ages of 16 to 24.

Table 1 Number of UK home pupils and students by education sector in 1987-88.

Sector	Pupils/students	Percentage of total
Schools	8,838,000	63
Further education	*4,033,000	30
Higher education	920,000	7
Total	13,311,000	100

* This includes 1,578,000 students aged 16 years or more in adult education centres.

[1] The latest figures (DES *et al*, 1989) available at the time of undertaking the work, summer 1990, and hence included here and below.

Table 2   Number of UK home students aged 16+ by education sector in 1987-88.

Sector	Pupils/students	Percentage of total
Schools	489,000	9
Further education	*4,033,000	74
Higher education	920,000	17
Total	5,442,000	100

*   This includes 1,578,000 students aged 16 years or more in adult education centres.

Table 3   Percentage of the UK young adult home population participating in education, 1987-88.*

Sector	Aged 16-18	Aged 19-20	Aged 21-24
Schools	18	-	-
Further education	33	13	12
Higher education	4	15	6

*   Includes YTS in public sector colleges but excludes private sector FE and in-company training.

However you view it, FE represents an enormous share of every cake: 30 per cent of all learners, 74 per cent of post-compulsory students (most, of course, part-time). Among those aged 16-18, FE attracts more than 1.8 times the school proportion. Among 19-20 years olds, FE provides for 46 per cent of all adults participating in education. Among 21-24 year olds it has twice as many students as HE. The overwhelming majority of adults who experience post-school public sector education and training do so in colleges of further education.

There are other impressive statistics. Approximately 41 per cent of all A level students are in FE (Baker, 1989), and more than 19 per cent of those who obtain A levels or SCE H grades acquire them through FE colleges (DES *et al*, 1989). FE is the major access route for non-traditional entry into higher education (HE). CFEs are reckoned to cost £2,000,000,000 a year, to employ 63,000 full-time (FT) lecturers. As Mr Baker observes (1989), 'It is a big, big enterprise'.

Nor do CFEs belong to the category of rare creatures, such as the unicorn or the yeti, much talked and written about but seldom or never seen. Most people have easy access to a college of further education. There are about 385 of them in England, 26 in Northern Ireland, 49 in Scotland and 40 in Wales, a total of around 500. Compared to UK school statistics (35,000 establishments, 26,000 primary or nursery, 5,000 secondary, over 500,000 teachers) the FE figures may not look remarkable, but then schools provide compulsory education, 11 years of it, for every member of the population. In the sphere where attendance is voluntary, FE's prolific abundance is comparatively even more significant: there are only 45 universities and 89 other public sector higher education institutions with corporate status in England and Wales, while CFEs number nearly 400.

The actual facts about FE are thus impressive. However, if Mr Baker is to be believed, FE's public image is quite the reverse, which points to a paradox. How is it possible for a significantly large part of a major public sector industry to be widely available and used by millions of people, while at the same time remaining largely invisible and frequently regarded as inconsequential? Is FE really the Cinderella of the education service, dowdy and low profile? If so, why? And how might it be made otherwise?

Confirming the assumption

Dramatic assertions should not go unquestioned, even (or perhaps especially) if we are inclined to agree. Mr Baker's conviction might well be jaundiced and ill-informed. In public, at least, ministers usually rely on empirical evidence of the statistical variety, carefully selected by advisers to dazzle voters and bewilder opponents. Mr Baker, however, had no access to statistics about how the average person perceives FE. Instead he offered only unsubstantiated allegations. I therefore set myself the task of trying to determine to what extent, if at all, the Baker hypothesis is valid. It led me to search for evidence intended to answer one fundamental question: What is the general public perception of FE?

At the same time, in the event that what I discovered should prove either sufficiently disturbing and/or negative to warrant additional investigation, I tackled three supplementary questions intended to explore possible means of alleviating any problems which my research might highlight.

- How do those responsible for projecting FE's image – marketing officers and college principals – believe their colleges of further education are viewed by the public?

- If the present situation is not acceptable, what kind of image should FE be striving to project?

- How can the desired image be achieved?

Collecting evidence

At a time when external funding has become enormously difficult to come by, intention and means do not always coincide for a researcher. One consequently learns to play the magpie and seek material wherever it surfaces, either by accident or through the kind agency of colleagues. A number of data sources have thus come to my attention fortuitously rather than by my own design. I have used anything and everything which seemed to shed light – however pale – on shadowy landscapes. In confronting a big question on a small budget, one welcomes any and all assistance.

Ideally I should have undertaken a large national poll of the kind with which politicians are familiar, but this was beyond the limited resources available to me. I adopted a more modest approach, expanding an interview schedule (see below) which formed part of another project, drawing upon relevant work I could find by other researchers, and looking for clues in material already in print but not necessarily intended to address my query.

One initiative aimed at facilitating FE image transformation is the FE Marketing Unit (itself endorsed in Mr Baker's speech), for which I worked on a feasibility study and business plan in the latter part of 1989 (Theodossin, 1989c) on a project jointly funded by The Staff College and DES. The purpose of the study was to test the viability of setting up a national FE marketing support agency and to identify what kinds of goods and services colleges might be prepared to buy. I interviewed college principals and college and LEA marketing officers, i.e. people who were potential Unit customers but whose roles also require them to operate at the interface between the college and the market-place, and who thus have many opportunities to judge how their colleges and colleagues are generally viewed.

In the interviews, I began by testing the Baker perception. Before asking about what kinds of goods and services they might consider buying from the Unit, I invited respondents to explore FE's image, how they believed it was perceived by different market segments, whether the prevalent image was satisfactory, how it ought to be modified (if at all) and what could be done to achieve any desired transformation. Sometimes respondents discoursed reflectively for a half hour or more before turning to potential purchasing needs. The responses were often startlingly frank, revealing beliefs and concerns that would not normally be made public, particularly by people whose jobs include responsibility for selling FE. The result is FE as seen from the inside by those who run it and know it best. The picture that emerges is remarkably honest and often deeply troubled.

Partly, one suspects, the views reflect a larger educational problem, the frequently noted demoralisation and demotivation of a service which has been subjected to repeated political and public scrutiny and admonishment for the past decade, and which is currently in the throes of externally imposed radical changes. For some years teaching has not been a comfortable occupation. Confidence has been undermined. Beliefs have been challenged. And perhaps most threatening, the protectionism and financial security which were once taken for granted have been eroded. Many of the interview responses must to some extent reflect anxieties which go beyond the public image of the service.

In order to respect the confidences of respondents, quotations from LEA and college staff in later pages are anonymous. The interview questions are discussed in the text and the research methodology is described in Appendix A.

Practitioner views represent only one part of the picture. In the summer and autumn of 1990 I undertook a search through a wide variety of published materials – newspapers, periodicals, college prospectuses, etc. – to explore how the press sees FE, how FE is represented at central government level, the extent to which FE is regularly researched, and how colleges present themselves to the public.

I have also drawn upon material collected during the Responsive College Programme (RCP), some of which has been published elsewhere (Theodossin, 1989a and 1989b) in a different form and for a different purpose, but the remainder of which was completed too late for inclusion in the Programme's dissemination package. RCP was an action programme intended to find out how to market individual colleges, while this book is concerned with the general cultural image and political position of FE: this has sometimes required looking at existing data from a slightly different perspective.

Chapter 2:
FE and the general public

At the heart of a marketing approach lies the maxim that effective selling is dependent on knowing the market-place and its inhabitants. Many US colleges therefore invest in attitude surveys. Their goal is to find out whether the college's public image serves the institution's interests, and if not, to devise ways of improving it. By way of illustration, in its marketing plan for 1987 (Fonte & Leach 1986), Chicago's Triton College records that

> Surveys conducted in spring '86 among...a representative sample of community residents showed that...80 per cent of the district residents rated Triton's general reputation as good or excellent. The percentage of community residents rating Triton's reputation as good or excellent was higher in 1986 than in 1980, when 77 per cent gave a good or excellent rating.

A histogram reveals that 1,000 residents were involved in the community survey. These respondents were not necessarily students of the college, but 'district residents' who might be expected to have views about the 'reputation' of community education in their localities.

Comparable longitudinal data about the perceptions of local people would be difficult to uncover in most of our colleges. Part of the reason may be resource limitations, but the more likely explanation derives from cultural differences.

Until recently, FE colleges have had limited formal autonomy in the conduct of their own affairs. They have been part of local authority provision, owned by the LEA and subject to imposed controls and regulations. Any single college has usually been one of a number of schools and colleges whose catchment areas and curriculum offerings overlap to some extent. In addition, many local educational services have been reorganised, amalgamated, merged and/or renamed, so that any one college (or school) has often been a temporary manifestation. This has not prevented individual establishments from having local reputations, but the authority's public and visible emphasis has been on the totality of its educational provision, rather than this school or that college.

At the same time, Britain has not traditionally been a consumer-orientated society. The average customer has tended to be compliant and disinclined to make a fuss. Compared to the more vociferous populations of other countries, we seldom write letters or organise public protests. We continue to rely heavily on journalists and watchdog bodies to expose provider deficiencies on our behalf. Professionals (including teachers) can expect litigation initiated by dissatisfied customers far less frequently than their North American counterparts. As customers, we may complain, but we generally do so out of the offender's hearing. Suppliers cannot therefore be blamed for showing little interest in spending money on researching our attitudes: they have a comparatively quiet life and want to keep it that way. Why expose complex and costly problems?

To some extent this is changing. The last decade has seen a central government push towards consumerism. In response, colleges have acknowledged, if not always embraced, marketing. Extended opening hours, single queues in banks and post offices, and interest paid on current account balances – provision long taken for granted elsewhere – are all fairly recent phenomena designed to improve the purchaser's lot. Sunday trading has still not reached the statute book, but the volume of infringements appears to be growing. Yet, in many respects Britain remains a conservative country and the battle to promote customer centredness is long, slow and uphill most of the way.

Thus regular and systematic scrutiny of public opinion has been slow to surface in Britain, and most of it has been associated with political parties, either private polls conducted by central office or the public kind paid for by national media for their own ends. As a result, week by week we know more about what the nation thinks of the Prime Minister and the Opposition Leader than we do about how those who live within our locality regard the services we all use regularly.

Customer surveys are used mainly in the private sector or by public sector providers facing privatisation, such as British Rail. Like colleges, local authorities have only recently begun to think of those they serve as 'customers'. Few of us can have been asked by the local authority to answer questions about what we think of our medical centres, car parks, roads, libraries, parks, schools and colleges. Most of us have views, but few people in positions of authority have bothered to canvass them.

Insider views of outsider views

Despite the absence in education of the kind of empirical data which polls and surveys produce, those occupying positions of authority in colleges usually hold views about how they and their organisations are regarded. Most perceptions derive from the unorganised accumulation of day-to-day personal experience. They are impressionistic, with little or no quantitative evidence, but they are nonetheless a useful starting point.

In the feasibility study survey (see Appendix A) previously noted, respondents – principals, vice-principals, assistant principals, marketing officers (LEA and college) – were asked, What image do you think FE has among individual customers – potential students (and their parents)? Some respondents advanced predominantly positive views.

> We are the place to go to. We link to HE and employment. We used to have a last-resort image. (Vice-principal)

> FE is the place to go for adult-type courses. There's a different atmosphere from what you get in schools and it offers wider opportunities. (Principal)

> This college has a high profile among 16 year olds. Some think they're not academic enough for us. (Principal)

> It's good. The city works hard at promoting its colleges. There are joint adverts and a high profile in the press. It works hard at publicity. (Principal)

> We're perceived as a slightly up-market college (College marketing officer)

Two principals saw FE as possessing a poor general image but their own colleges as exceptions.

> In this locality we're seen as equal to a sixth form college. In the town where I used to work FE was a poor relation. (Principal)

> Until recently ordinary members of the community had a poor image of FE. Locally – at least in this area – people are fully aware of the service. But in general, at regional and national levels, FE has a poor image. (Principal)

As might have been anticipated, no respondent offered evidence of any form of attitude survey undertaken by the college. Even with such data it would be difficult to describe local people as 'fully aware' of the service, as the last respondent did. One attempt to circumvent the problem involved another principal using enrolment figures as a crude proxy of customer approval.

> We've got a good image. Our FT intake has been increasing for the last four years despite the demographic trend. We're an A level success story. This year we've had 573 enrolments, largely A levels, and that's up from 520 last year. And we're in an area with a 47 per cent staying on rate, so we've done very well. Adult education is well established, but I'm not convinced it's offering the courses people need. We haven't changed our adult education courses in five years, and it's beginning to show in reduced intake. (Principal)

Such fundamentally positive observations – qualified or not – were in the minority. At the other extreme, there were many more respondents who saw FE as possessing a wholly or partially negative image. One group could see little from which FE staff could draw comfort.

> ...wide range of courses...variable quality in terms of delivery...appalling administration...bad customer relations...dated in content (especially high technology)...not particularly good accommodation... (Assistant principal, marketing)

> People would prefer better accommodation, getting rid of the matchstick furniture and a better paint job. (Principal)

> It's not favourable. The words that come to mind are intimidating, confusing, grubby, a 16-18 environment. In grammar schools FE is seen as a second choice. In comprehensives, less than high achievers regard us as the place where clever people go. (LEA marketing officer)

> The image is relatively poor across most sectors. We're not held in high regard, except for the traditional training of youngsters. It's an uphill struggle to be seen as a serious provider of training of the more focused sort. (Assistant principal, marketing)

> For some it's the only option (technical education). For others it's the place where they can go part-time (the bulk). For still others it's the alternative to higher education, to getting qualifications in some other way. FE doesn't really meet student needs. It doesn't provide

a high enough quality environment. It doesn't treat students well enough. (College marketing officer)

It's not the correct image. We're thought of as poorer than we're entitled to be. We're well known and thought of in some instances. (Assistant principal, marketing)

As with the more positive views quoted above, these respondents offered no evidence other than their own subjective assessments.

Others challenged the question itself. These people asserted – as some of the above respondents had implied – that there was not one, but a variety of images, depending on who was doing the viewing.

All adult education and recreational courses are provided through colleges in this LEA. So we are used by the community, and in this particular area – with an unemployment rate of three per cent – we have a large number of people who can afford to pay for leisure courses. Beyond that, something of a tech approach is still there in the minds of older people, although not among younger members of the community. But most people think of FE as a college which provides an opportunity for a second chance at all ages. (Principal)

There's no straightforward answer. It depends on their contact with FE. (Principal)

It's varied. It depends on their age, their aspirations ...whether they're on YTS or doing an HE course... (Principal)

The majority of the multiple-image group, however, depicted a plurality of views of which few could be described as flattering. Their general impression was of a clear lack of public enthusiasm, of a service which was at best reluctantly accepted rather than positively embraced.

Our image with the vast majority of younger people is in terms of crafts, construction, engineering – or a way of resitting academic qualifications. The more traditional older groups think of evening classes, recreational work: what will we do this year? (Principal)

It depends on the students. In schools we're not seen as too bad. In HE (we do some courses) you get bad comments: 'We don't want to speak to them'. We're really seen as a second-class, last resort. (College marketing officer)

For young people, FE is the second chance. You go if you can't get into a polytechnic or university. You go to do YTS. For older people, FE is the tech and evening classes and apprenticeships, that they remember from their youth. (Principal)

For some people it's seen as threatening and big. There's a segment that like that. Others see it as non-academic, despite the A level programme. Others see it as a convenient local facility. (Assistant principal)

It depends on the area of work. In specialist areas where the competition is not so good we're seen as bright. There are those who think of us as a tech with a high profile and a good image. It's not quite so good for general education. We can be seen as the place for people who had trouble at school, for repeaters – and our results are not as good as at a sixth form college. (Principal)

Invisibility and confusion

Another group of respondents stressed not the positive or negative image held by members of the community, but the lack of any image whatsoever for a significantly large proportion of the public. Five respondents believed that CFEs – like Chesterton's postman – were often invisible.

Among younger and more academic customers, there's a negative image of the tech: sex and drugs and rock and roll – not such a nice place to study. Among the general public it's an image of flower arranging. But to many people we're still invisible: our existence isn't relevant to them. (Associate vice-principal, marketing)

The majority are singularly unaware of FE and what it can do for them. Those who know about us generally think of FE as for losers, a second-rate place. (Principal)

The image is non-existent for people who have no experience of FE. (Principal)

Many people do not know the college. (College marketing officer)

We've done quite a lot to raise our image, but I suspect we've probably raised it more with FE than with the public. (Principal of a college well known in the FE world for its innovative marketing)

Eight others emphasised what they viewed as widespread public confusion about FE.

> A low and confusing image. I do talk to fifth year youngsters and parents because I enjoy doing it. I see the glazed look in their eyes. They don't know what we do. Parents have done day release courses but they have little idea of what else we do. Schools careers staff change so rapidly. We have several buildings, many departments. (Principal)

> The image is vague. It's not clear as it is with polytechnics and colleges. (College publicity officer)

> It's confused. There's no clear picture of how FE relates. It's the catch-all. It's where you go if you can't find anywhere else. It's not a positive image offering anything particular. In inner cities it's a second chance. (Principal)

> I don't know that individual customers are clear about what FE is. They know about schools and universities, but colleges of FE are something of a mystery in relation to HE colleges and polys. (Principal)

> We're a large, all-through FE college with a nearby HE college. This confuses the public. Also adult education can be linked, although that isn't the case here. The basic problem is that FE is trying to be all things to all people. No one – even students – grasps the whole range of provision. We're looking at a segmentation approach. There's a need to identify client groups and to address their needs individually. (Vice-principal, marketing)

> People are unsure as to what happens behind the doors. If they're new to colleges, they think it's a university and not for them. We don't know what to do about it. We have to work on the problem. (Principal)

> Where there's direct contact, the image is quite good. There are still many people who don't know what's on. They have a vague idea about 'night school'. The opinion is formed by looking at the building. It's an 'institution' and not for them. (Principal)

There's a better awareness now than 20 to 30 years ago. It's not a high profile. Everyone knows about schools. Most people know about a university. They're vague about FE. 25 years ago we had business and engineering apprentices, we did craft and vocational work. A lot has had to change. Because the identity has changed, people don't know what we do. There are now a lot of private agencies in our business. (Principal)

There were inevitably some respondents who could not resist blaming public confusion – and much more besides – on other people both inside and outside the college, i.e. hostile or unthinking individuals allegedly responsible for college problems.

It's totally varied. It depends on the locality. Here they still think of the college as a tech where you do what you can't do at school. This view is reinforced by school teachers and perpetuated by the careers service, even though they're independent. (Principal)

Those who know about it think it's very important. It gives access to HE. But the awareness is local, limited, ad hoc, accidental. Outside, people are indifferent. They have no opinions. The politicians on the education committee see us as peripheral, with staff who are overpaid, unresponsive and very cushy. (Principal)

In this area we have a user-friendly image which is constantly being chipped away at by unthinking front-line staff and by cuts. (Principal)

It's reasonably good among our traditional client groups, i.e. school leavers. But careers and guidance staff are confused about food and catering. We compete with central institutions who are better resourced. Over 12 years we've achieved something, but at careers conventions, compared with high calibre providers, we don't come out very well. (Scottish principal)

Are others really at fault? Are colleges the victims of prejudiced, unthinking and uncaring school teachers, careers advisers, education committees, politicians and CFE staff? If so, one might legitimately ask what the college is doing to change either the detractors' and/or the public's attitudes.

A High Street perspective

There are exceptions to the generalisation offered above about the absence of college market-place data. In RCP some projects gathered evidence from particular customer groups (e.g. school leavers and employers, both discussed below), and on occasion college students have conducted attitude surveys as part of their course project work. This work tended to be carried out as a one-off, discrete activity, rather than as part of a longitudinal survey designed to reveal changes in public attitudes. Nor was any of this work necessarily linked to properly resourced management attempts to modify general perceptions.

To my knowledge, only one college – here given the fictitious name of Benson College – has employed a market research firm to conduct a series of interviews with local residents and to ask them about the college: what it did; where it was; whether it met the educational needs of local people. Benson is a split-site institution in an inner city area where it serves a multi-ethnic, working-class population.

The survey results derive from an opportunity sample culled from those who happened to be passing an interviewer stationed on the High Street pavement. They give a useful insight into how at least some people perceive Benson. One notes the association of colleges with young people and with schools in the community mind, places which might lead to a job but which can be ignored by those in work, not altogether surprising when one remembers that most CFEs have grown from either mechanics institutes or technical schools. At no point is there anything which could be construed as enthusiasm. There is a substantial amount of confusion about the college's various sites, no doubt exacerbated by a recent amalgamation.

> Yes, I know where the college is. I go past in the bus many times. It's near the police station. It's very big and there's building going on at the moment. I didn't know there were other centres. With three little ones I'm not really interested in colleges. If there is a place for the children maybe I would go. I don't know. Wouldn't it be just for very young people? (Female, aged 19, married with three children)

> Someone comes in and puts the odd leaflet up on the board advertising some of the courses but I don't really know that much about the college. I wouldn't have thought there were five centres. People usually go to whichever one is nearest, I suppose. Do they have different classes in each one? (Female helper at a local church centre)

I've got a thing telling you all about the courses at Benson College because my aunt is pushing me to do things. I haven't seen the college yet...I've been told there's a lot of fights that break out there and that teachers have been attacked. Sounds like a prison. (Male, aged 18, unemployed and at present living with his aunt because of problems at home)

It's so bleak and dark somehow – very depressing. But once you're inside, it's a friendly atmosphere. (Female, aged 22, unemployed and at present living with her boyfriend)

That's actually Benson College, is it? I knew it was a college but I wasn't sure of its name. It looks a bit grim to me. I hated school, so I'm glad to be away from those places, having lessons rammed down your throat. I don't know what they actually do there but I'm sure it's the sort of stuff you do at school, English and all that. I'm pretty lucky having a job, so I don't really think about it, although I wouldn't want to work in here all my life. (Male, aged 23, who works for a newsagent)

General, shorter comments from the survey reinforce the widespread impression of physical unattractiveness.

It's just a bit further up the road on the left. It's a bit dark and boarded up.

It's that big place next door to the police station.

It's that ugly building, you know, all modern like, just across the road from the library.

By way of explication one needs to note there are valid reasons for such unattractiveness: years of under-funding, inadequate building programmes and 'soft' cuts in upkeep and maintenance in preference to 'hard' cuts in staffing have taken their toll. Beyond the squalid decor there is also in Benson a special characteristic of many large institutions, the presence everywhere of injunctions and instructions which create an atmosphere of prohibitive restraint. One can see this very clearly in a photographic collage put together by the market research firm, wherein can be found a wide range of commands (those which follow are a sample) more redolent of a motorway or a remand centre than an educational establishment.

–   Staff only,

- Keep clear,

- Danger! Guard dogs patrolling,

- All passes must be shown,

- Please show your student pass to security guard.

No one could accuse Benson CFE of trusting its customers, and presumably they respond by doing their best to justify the college's lack of confidence.

An interesting point is that not only do most European and North American colleges not feel the need to make the general public feel quite so unwelcome by providing comparable commands and prohibitions, but Benson's own students presumably use shops and cinemas, public transport and restaurants, churches and temples, where they do not need to run the gauntlet of guard dogs or establish their identity with passes.

Of course, the Benson data is untypical. The college is one of those inner-city institutions which labour under a variety of exceptional difficulties: a population suffering from many social and economic disadvantages and thus greatly in need of support from a local authority struggling to balance its budget; built-up sites without sufficient open land to soften the harsh institutional image; no parking facilities for the public; racial tension; a need for dramatic investment in fabric and furnishings; and so on. Most colleges still do not employ security guards and dogs. The many difficulties which Benson presents to those who manage it probably account for the interest in a public survey: it is usually when things seem to be going badly that one seeks confirmation and explanation.

Images are not immutable

Apart from Benson, we possess very little direct and reliable data about how the average man in the supermarket or the women in the bus queue views FE colleges. No one seems to have possessed both the interest and the means to collect such information from a representative example across the country. We rely, therefore, on reflected images.

The general impression created by the admittedly fragmentary and limited evidence from college managers and Benson citizens is of a service which may sometimes be perceived positively, but is too often viewed otherwise. The public frequently regard it as down-market, second choice and sometimes second best. The physical plant is not very attractive. Different market segments perceive it variously (sometimes approvingly, sometimes not), but many are confused about what it does and provides, and sometimes about where it is. To extend Mr Baker's epithet, FE can be 'low profile' to the point of being indiscernible. FE has an image problem.

In some ways, the feasibility study evidence from FE managers and marketeers is even harder on FE than are the passers by in Benson High Street. The latter appear largely indifferent, unenthusiastic rather than overtly hostile. They are, after all, uninterested pedestrians who have been stopped while going about their own business. By contrast, the college senior staff are better educated, more widely experienced and capable of using language more incisively. They also know the problems more fully because they deal with them daily, and their negative observations are thus more trenchant and disturbing.

What also surfaces in many of the professional observations is a Cinderella-like low level of self-esteem and a pervading sense of defeat. If valuing oneself is a necessary condition for caring about others, these respondents too often seem to have doubts about the worth of what they offer and lack confidence in its intrinsic attractiveness to customers.

The image problem is thus not solely about how the public perceives FE, but also about how those who work in it regard both themselves and their colleges. Images are ephemeral, not fixed. They can be changed.

A familiar textbook example of dramatic image modification involves Japanese manufacturing industry. Before the Second World War, Japanese goods were regarded as cheap and shoddy. Today they are widely perceived as expensive, high quality luxury products, both technologically advanced and reliable in performance. This transformation was achieved within a short period by deliberate policy changes and promotional campaigns. If a country can improve its position in the world market-place, why not a college in its local catchment area? Images are not immutable.

Chapter 3:
The major FE markets

The promotional problems which face FE derive from its work profile. **Table 4** sets out statistics on UK FE students from home and abroad by type of course and mode of study. In terms of student numbers, the three largest recruiting areas are: GCE, GCSE, SCE and CSE; administration, business and social studies; and engineering and technology. As pure headcounts, the figures are misleading. Part-time students need to be calculated in terms of full-time equivalents if they are to make any quantitative sense. Engineering has been declining for some years, while technology (particularly the information variety) has been growing.

Such caveats aside, what is readily apparent is that for FE colleges GCE, GCSE, SCE and CSE represent the area of business which recruits the largest number of full-time students (it takes several part-timers to make up the teaching equivalent of one full-time student). The remaining FE work is dominated by vocational training. Both these facts go a long way towards explaining why many FE colleges concentrate their marketing and promotional efforts on school leavers and employers: both are major customer groups and lucrative lines of business.

The tense relationship between schools and colleges

Most CFEs make strenuous efforts to promote themselves positively with school leavers: running link courses to enable pupils to experience the range of college provision; holding open days; producing videos and slide presentations for use in schools; attending school careers conventions; and so on. For many colleges, school leavers are a market upon whose effective penetration institutional survival depends.

And yet – despite college efforts – the relationship with school leavers remains equivocal. Some schools are known to block visits from college staff whom they regard as competitors trying to poach pupils. Others are reputed to throw out college promotional literature directed at pupils. In one of the RCP projects, school headteachers succeeded for a year in withholding pupil home addresses,

Table 4. FE students from home and abroad by type of course and mode of study, 1987-88.

Subject group	Full-time	Part-time
Education	7,400	14,000
Medicine, dentistry and health	18,800	25,300
Engineering and technology	56,900	302,900
Agriculture, forestry and veterinary science	5,800	26,600
Science	13,100	33,500
Administration, business and social studies	78,300	284,800
Architecture and other professional and vocational subjects	64,900	146,100
Languages, literature and area studies	1,600	29,000
Arts other than languages	4,000	65,200
Music, drama, art and design	29,400	39,600
GCE, GCSE, SCE and CSE	103,700	274,300
Other	37,600	384,900
Total	421,500	1626,200

thus frustrating local authority attempts to inform school leavers of the range of education and training opportunities in the county. There is a long history of unease in contacts between schools and colleges.

In recent years, school-college tension has increased as the demographic downturn has led to declining school intakes. Market contraction has stimulated fierce competition. The political difficulties LEAs experienced in trying to rationalise provision may be seen as one main reason why Government gave colleges devolved financial control and pushed them into the market-place, where it is hoped consumers will resolve the over-provision problem.

Historically it was colleges who first encroached on the school market by providing alternative examination courses for young people who did not wish to remain in school after the age of 16, and for adults who wanted to return to study. This school-college overlap has been one of the defining characteristics of CFEs, distinguishing them from comparable institutions in other countries, where the break between school and post-compulsory education is marked by clear institutional differentiation.

The overlap creates FE marketing and promotional problems because it links CFEs to schools and prevents FE from providing a portfolio consisting only of distinctive offerings. An organisation which has a precisely defined image and a limited product range – like Mothercare or the Royal Opera House – is easier to market than one which, like FE, offers a bit of everything. The attempt to rationalise the situation by producing tertiary colleges has won its adherents, but it has also long since run up against political constraints which have limited its progress. Among non-professionals, tertiary colleges – together with mushrooming sixth forms, sixth form colleges and consortia – have served to confuse the general public still more.

At present the problem is growing. Schools have begun to penetrate new post-compulsory markets. They increasingly offer vocational courses, and in some instances have been franchised by colleges to provide BTEC qualifications. In Scotland schools advertise in-fill provision for adults. The 1991 FE White Paper proposes that schools in England and Wales should do the same.

FE, having shed much of its HE to a new incorporated system, has begun to seek the franchise for the early years of undergraduate work, an arrangement which over-recruiting HE institutions have been keen to promote. Anyone in search of a neat and tidy education system must learn to accommodate growing diversity, duplicate provision and encroachment, until or unless the local market identifies winners and losers.

In some instances individual CFEs have chosen to phase out examination work aimed at HE entry and have committed themselves entirely to vocational courses, but such colleges are in a minority. The majority are too dependent on GCE, GCSE, SCE and CSE to abandon this market altogether. As a result, school-college tensions are likely to increase over the next few years.

FE colleges and school leavers

Despite (or perhaps because of) the difficulties which CFEs often experience in recruiting from local schools, school leavers are probably the market which colleges understand most fully and in which they are most accurately perceived by potential customers. Schools are also a market which colleges have researched extensively, partly because it is so important in terms of numbers, but also because school pupils (once the headteacher's approval has been obtained) represent a large captive audience prepared to fill in even the most lengthy questionnaires.

Four RCP projects made forays into local schools to find out what pupils thought of CFEs. One (Bedfordshire RCP, 1986) questionnaired 160 fourth formers about to enter the fifth form to learn how they viewed local colleges. Only three per cent had visited a college, but four-fifths said they would consider applying for a college course. More than half saw colleges as providing courses with vocational qualifications which gave the holder an employment advantage.

In Suffolk (Pardey, 1987), with 'the lowest 1984 college staying-on rate of all shire counties', the RCP project conducted 'extensive open-ended discussions' with small groups drawn from 71 first-year students at four county colleges and a further questionnaire to 249 pupils in six local authority schools. Colleges were seen as accessible and not too off-putting, but also as not providing as much student support as schools.

The Gwynedd (Dunkin, 1987) project surveyed the entire fifth year at one local authority school. Female pupils were more satisfied with their knowledge of FE than were males. Both sexes relied on careers teachers for information, but the second source was college open days for females and the county careers service for males. Males and females visited colleges equally, but males tended to arrive in school groups while females organised their own visits. Impressions formed during informal visits with parents were worse than those gained during organised school tours.

A Lancashire study (Undergraduates of Lancaster University, Department of Marketing, 1988) visited five of a single college's seven feeder schools. 16 focus group interviews were conducted with 99 students, who also completed questionnaires. The results showed a mixture of positive and negative impressions. On the plus side, it was widely believed that the college was biased towards vocational work and that students were treated as adults and had a varied choice of courses. More than half thought the college had good facilities. Some courses – including secretarial studies, business and finance, and motor vehicle studies – had better reputations than others. Conversely, many respondents felt that studying A levels in the sixth form was preferable to doing so at the college: sixth forms had better reputations academically. The school leavers complained about leaflets containing only limited information and about the lack of visits by college staff to their schools (which may not have been the college's fault).

None of these findings could be described as devastating. Colleges aim to be, and are, different from schools: that each should be perceived as possessing distinctive advantages and disadvantages is understandable. Because CFEs compete with schools on the latter's home ground, the fact that so many pupil respondents were relatively positive suggests that CFE efforts had overcome any teacher opposition. The Gwynedd evidence also shows that colleges are capable of organising effective visits for schools, even if they are less impressive when caught on the hop.

Even if CFEs cannot feel entirely confident about school leaver perceptions, and certainly cannot afford to reduce their recruitment efforts, this is one market about which colleges ought to feel both confident and comfortable. It is also likely that colleges represent more of a threat to schools than the reverse.

It was therefore somewhat surprising to find that feasibility study respondents more often than not stressed the negative perceptions of school leavers. Three marketing officers – all closely involved with school recruitment – emphasised the less positive aspects in interviews, even if they doubtless did the reverse on selling expeditions.

> There is a strand who see us as the second option. We have strong sixth forms locally. We can be seen as a place for adults. Schools here are less competitive with us than in other areas, but it's an uphill fight to get people to recognise the value of BTEC. We run evening advice sessions from Christmas to the summer term and work hard to talk second chance A level applicants into BTEC. (College marketing officer)

> With school leavers it depends on what school they went to. If it's a school with a sixth form, we're seen as places with shady, poorly qualified people and poorly equipped laboratories. If it's a school without a sixth form, we're viewed as interesting, a place where people are treated as adults. (College marketing officer)

> The 16+ market sees us as the vocational route, a second chance, an alternative to school (especially if they don't like it). (College marketing officer)

> Greater confidence seemed to surface only when competition was absent.

We're a community college with a theatre, an adult institute. In our area, 16+ youngsters really have no choice. (College marketing officer)

The 16-19 age groups sees us as an alternative, but for some there is no alternative. (College marketing officer)

One respondent raised the problem of invisibility brought on by LEA reorganisation, doubtless regarded by the organisers as a means of improving provision, but viewed by the public as bewildering.

We're in a new merger situation. We've done lots of PR and publicity and made personal contacts. We believe the image has improved, but we're not yet able to say whether it has been transcribed into extra students. Part of the exercise has been awareness raising, but we still get people asking, What? (Principal)

Altogether, there was little in either the extensive RCP research or the feasibility study interviews to suggest that CFEs face major marketing problems in schools, apart from those created for them by anxious competitors or well intentioned bureaucrats bent on reorganisation. No one has ever claimed that CFEs are eager to do anything other than lure school leavers to college courses, or that they are generally other than successful at the task.

RCP evidence about colleges and employers

From the early 1980s onwards, CFEs came under steady criticism from Government for their alleged deficiencies in serving the needs of industry. Training for jobs (DE/DES, 1984) accused them of being unresponsive and aroused enormous hostility from both colleges and LEAs. Competence and competition (NEDO/ MSC, 1984) encouraged them to market rather than sell their services.

Money was made available to foster an improved relationship between colleges and employers. The DES ran the College-Employer Links Project to explore how employers could make a fuller contribution to the running of college advisory committees. The Manpower Services Commission funded hundreds of local collaborative projects to stimulate closer links between educational establishments and employers. Although its remit was somewhat broadened at a latter stage, RCP started life as an attempt to find ways of enabling colleges to meet employer needs more successfully.

That there was a a college-employer problem was corroborated over and over in RCP project work. Although Gwynedd engineering firms (50 interviews, 70 completed questionnaires) praised lecturing staff, only a third thought colleges were providing a good service (Jones and Dunkin, 1987). Among respondents from 50 Sheffield engineering firms, about a third would regularly contact colleges for help with a training problem, but similar proportions would do so either sometimes or never (Crowson and Chapman, 1987).

The Strathclyde Project (Howie and Traynor, 1987) questioned 154 college employer users (49 returns) and learned that nearly 90 per cent carried out in-house training and almost two-thirds used private providers. Although 40 per cent had visited colleges during the previous year, only 30 per cent claimed to have been visited by college staff.

In a massive survey of engineering firms in the local area (questionnaire data from 871 firms and in-depth follow-up interviews with 277 respondents), the Dudley project (Doherty and Woodhall, 1987) found that colleges were viewed as not providing relevant courses, as having out-of-date equipment and staff, as unresponsive, uncommunicative and unwilling to listen to industrialists. Colleges were rarely mentioned in any positive way and private training agents were noted more often than colleges and were more highly rated as contributors to training.

A fifth project (Theodossin, 1989a), which requested anonymity for its findings, interviewed 150 employers running small businesses.

Their complaints about the LEA's five colleges stressed the difficulties of making contact with colleges: prolonged telephone ringing, telephonists unaware of the details of any course, the unavailability of anyone to answer the caller's questions, leaving messages which took days for a response or were never acknowledged. The overall picture was persistently negative and far more critical than anything which was revealed among school leavers.

Responding to employer training demands

RCP belonged to the second half of the 1980s. One might therefore ask how in the seven years since Training for jobs (DE/DES, 1984) confronted CFEs, college-employer relations might have altered, or at least whether college managers and marketeers themselves see their institutions' relations with industry improving. In the feasibility study, 62 respondents were asked, What image do you think FE has among employers?

Respondents were almost equally divided between those who believed relations had improved and those who did not, which may in itself be a fairly good indication of considerable change. There were no exaggerated claims of having achieved a miraculous transformation. Instead, these respondents stressed the evolving situation and the major improvements made.

> It's very good now. We're seen as very co-operative. We have a partnership with industry. (Vice-principal)

> Some see us as a valuable resource, as an approved training organisation. (College marketing officer)

> It's quite good. It must be if they keep sending students here. (Principal)

> Their view of FE is improving. Five years ago it probably wasn't as good as it should have been. Much has been done to improve the image. (Principal)

> It's changing. Locally there's been a shift in perception. We've been doing work with employers. We've become more responsive. We've been marketing. We put on short, customised courses. Those who don't come see us as unresponsive and rigid. (Principal)

> The image is improving. Numbers indicate this. It's an alternative to private providers. (College marketing officer)

> We have a better image with employers than in schools. Employers are involved in advisory committees. We have to work at it. Our image needs pushing much more professionally. (Principal)

Some respondents felt that there was no consistent employer view, that CFEs were regarded differently by different business people. The only safe generalisation was that one could not generalise with confidence. This group pointed to the inaccurate views held by some employers, frequently because of ignorance.

> The employers are very mixed in a town like this. We have courted some new companies, but there are a helluva lot who know little about us. They only send people on traditional courses when there's a skill shortage, so many middle size and small companies know nothing about us. (Principal)

> If the employer has been using us, he may realise our worth. We're now going out and putting on tailored courses. When we talk to employers they sometimes ask us, tongue in cheek, 'Do you think you can provide a professional service?' We have to prove ourselves. (College marketing officer)

Across the board it's still patchy. There's more work to be done, but in some specialist areas we have a great deal of support. (Principal) Our college has a good image. There are services we provide nationally. It depends on the links. Those employers who don't have a link might perceive us as old-fashioned and out of date. When I was in industry I was appalled. I thought of FE as way behind the times. The staff, too. (Principal)

There is not a view. Some from the printing industry have a positive view of us. Probably no one has a glowing, thrusting, dynamic view...except principals. (Principal)

It's changing, but small employers still see us as an extension of schooling. (Principal)

It's not so good, but it's getting better. Employers look upon us as the old tech where you learn basic manual skills. They don't realise that we have much more on offer. They still get surprised: 'I thought you just do welding'. We still get seen as a place that provides basket weaving, or Spanish for Majorca. (College marketing officer)

The latter respondent voiced a frustration felt by several others, that employers hold views which are uninformed and out of date. Colleges have changed, but some employers are unaware.

There's a gap. They see us as mainly City and Guilds and BTEC qualifications. That view may be out of date. (Principal)

They think we offer courses in the nine-to-five slot. They're surprised that we can fit in times to suit their shift patterns. (Principal)

Business people don't know what we do. (College publicity officer)

I know people in the chamber of commerce who have a disparaging view but who have had no contact with FE. (Principal)

They're still besotted with the concept of our not being as flexible as we should. We're a 48-week-a-year college. We sent out brochures to industry offering a modular pick-and-mix assortment, but after 18 months the response is still minimal. That's why I've moved towards the idea of door knocking for a year or two. (Principal)

The latter observation is very much to the point: customers are not obliged to keep themselves accurately informed about suppliers. Few of them feel any compunction to read all brochures which arrive in the post, and only large employers are likely to possess the luxury of a training officer whose job involves keeping abreast of current developments. Consequently any move towards 'door knocking' could make a significant difference.

The other side of the updating problem was neatly summed up by a principal.

> The big hotels change managers so quickly it's difficult to keep up with what's happening. We need to get out and find out what's happening. (Principal)

Employer-college relationships are double sided. In a world of rapid change everyone has difficulty in keeping abreast of outside developments.

Several respondents voiced the familiar complaint that employers are unclear about what they want.

> With big employers our image is quite good. They know what they want. Smaller employers don't know to come through the principal. Smaller employers think they can do as well themselves, or don't know what they want. (Principal)

> They don't always realise changes are taking place. They want quality, but they don't always know what they're looking for. (Principal)

The relative paucity of such complaints suggests that colleges have accepted that customers are not obliged to know what they want and that part of the supplier's role involves helping customers to identify needs.

There were also some complaints about employers. A community college principal felt that local industry was not always sympathetic to 'community orientated activities'. However, for many of these respondents more than half a decade of government pressure, public debate and changing college attitudes had developed the idea that if the college-employer relationship is not satisfactory, the college is fundamentally responsible for doing something about it.

A willingness to accept such responsibility was evident in the responses of a significantly large group of respondents who saw the variety of college-employer relationships as a consequence not of different employer perceptions, but of varying levels of competence among different sections of the college.

Hopefully it's improving. Our image is good in the high tech area, administration and clerical, basic engineering...we're strong in YTS and ET (they've both helped a lot), but we've got a long way to go. (Principal)

It depends on the individuals in individual colleges. (LEA marketing officer)

It's improving. We're anxious to get out to them and improve communications. Some departments are sophisticated. Others are not well advanced. One major contact, a chamber of commerce manager, said that improvements in colleges are quite noticeable. (Principal)

Building bridges is not easy work. The general impression left by these respondents was that most accepted the difficulties and believed that positive changes had occurred, but were prepared to acknowledge that more needed to be, and would be, done.

Market segmentation and differentiation

Another group of respondents, however, was convinced that what employers thought of colleges was anything but good news. At their most pessimistic, these interviewees depicted employer views as totally negative, and colleges as places which any sensible person would want to avoid.

Generally, it's not terribly good. (Principal)

Some firms use us for training, but there's a propensity to seek alternative training. (Principal)

It's not all that high. We're not highly regarded. (Principal)

Employers don't regard us as flexible or responsive in terms of delivery. They can't afford the time to send employees. They see our training as not relevant to their business plans. (College marketing officer)

Occasionally there were hints of something respectable, of rare exceptions among the general dross.

As out of touch places for academics, inflexible and only capable of dealing with certain types of training – with one or two excellent exceptions. (LEA marketing officer)

Flexibility isn't a word that would come to the lips of many employers. (Principal)

...good for standard, off-the-shelf packages...good in terms of the intellectual ability of the staff, but they need updating...badly organised, inflexible, wasteful ...lots of potential which can't be marshalled because of outdated working practices...outdated machinery and equipment...relatively cheap...bad publicity... (Assistant principal, marketing)

Such responses were not commonplace, but their rarity did not mitigate the concern that there are people in key positions in the FE service who either generally or in a moment of exceptional frankness, are prepared to criticise it (or their colleges) more fiercely than most of its external detractors.

The majority of respondents who believed employers had a negative image of CFEs were far less sweeping in their condemnations. Indeed, their comments centred on two very distinct criticisms.

1. Colleges are perceived as down market enterprises.

The poorer end of the scale in training – something that can be got cheaply. (College marketing officer)

FE is seen by companies as cheap and cheerful. (Assistant principal)

2. FE is considered appropriate only for apprentices.

They consider us OK for apprentices, 16-19 year olds. They wouldn't use us for updating. We're down-market. (Principal)

A large number see us as a place for apprentices... still...unfortunately. (Principal)

We're seen as the tech, where you get apprentice-level training – even if there are no apprentices. (College marketing officer)

Both perceptions are summed up by another principal.

I suppose we have a fair image. We're seen as doing a fair job for craft and technician training, but we're also seen as slow and inflexible. It's not a very up-beat image. The notion of 'dirty' FE still prevails. (Principal)

The notion is to some degree understandable. Historically, colleges have been down-market operations associated with apprenticeship training, i.e. with the production of blue- rather than white-collar workers.

It would be a mistake, however, to assume that this is unalterable and that nothing has changed. In some colleges substantial efforts have been made to develop new markets. If any college is to move up-market it will almost certainly need to transform its image, by running courses either in the workplace (which by definition defines the expectations of the workforce) or in attractive hotels and conference centres. Alternatively, it can invest in a special wing or building on its own premises in which superior provision is available for an enhanced charge, something approximating more closely to the boardroom than to the student union lounge. For the college, up-market means working with adults (including senior managers) and accepting that new and different market segments will have different, more costly and more demanding needs and expectations.

Up-market also leads us to a major promotional problem which many colleges have not yet addressed seriously. Those respondents who note varied employer perceptions of different sections of the college are taking what is largely a college managerial view, segmentation by curriculum area – catering, engineering, hairdressing. A marketing and promotional perspective emphasises another kind of differentiation, one based on customer status and purchasing ability. The training of middle and senior managers in catering is likely to have more in common with other areas of management training than with introductory catering courses. This is not to suggest that there are no differences in occupational culture, but rather to emphasise that such differences are not always of major significance in college promotional activity.

In marketing and promotion, customer segmentation is all. Diversity and variation are significant only insofar as they derive from market-place perceptions. In order to sell our offerings successfully, we must respond to the world not as we have known it or wish it to be, but to the world as seen by our customers.

It is possible that school leavers may be amenable to being treated as a homogeneous group, even if some are GCSE repeaters while others are starting A level courses. Whether undergraduates on franchised degree courses want to be grouped with school leavers is more doubtful. Similarly with employers, craft and technician training on the one hand and updating and management training on the other point us towards quite different delivery expectations. Colleges serve many distinctive markets, whose number and variety are growing. At the same time the need for differentiation in promotion and delivery is also increasing.

We talk to and interact differently with children, pets, lovers, colleagues, friends, parents and strangers. It is therefore inexplicable that we should expect to promote 'the college' in precisely the same way to a cornucopia of customers.

Chapter 4:
FE, government and the
national media

The quotations collected during the feasibility study and reproduced above indicate how senior staff in the FE system believe the outside world views their colleges, rather than how outsiders necessarily perceive FE colleges. Those respondents who believe that FE is seen negatively in the market-place use an assortment of words and phrases to describe the alleged vision: vague, confused, mystery, peripheral, non-existent image, not very sharp, a very grey area...and so on. How valid are such claims?

Those who insist that the above epithets are only too accurate offer various explanations. Everyone has been to school, but very few major decision makers have had any experience of FE as learners. Most staff holding senior posts in FE are graduates who have come through a different route and who are disinclined to encourage their own children to use the local college. Very few Members of Parliament or Cabinet Ministers have been in – never mind to – an FE college.

Graduates identify with HE, the institutions which awarded them their degrees rather than the colleges which helped them to gain entry to the degree course even if 19 per cent of those who obtain A levels or SCE H grades acquire them through FE colleges. The general public has no knowledge of or interest in FE. And so on... Is FE really – as I suggested in the opening chapter – education's invisible man?

A major national survey was clearly not within the scope of the present study, but there are performance indicators to which one can turn for some impression of how the general public views FE, and, perhaps more appropriately, how FE is presented to it. For example, does FE ever make news? Is FE a political issue? Does FE matter to people in education who do not work within FE? Education itself is of very considerable political interest and importance. All major political parties have much to say about what is wrong with – or ought to be put right in – our education system, and there is a seemingly perpetual debate about whether educational standards are falling or rising. In the summer of 1990, for example, Sir Claus Moser, Warden of Wadham College, Oxford, and a former head of the Government's statistical service, called for a royal commission on education that would be all-embracing and visionary, yet realistic. He noted (The Times, 21 August) that

> It is estimated that something like one child in seven leaves school functionally illiterate; some authorities' estimates put the figures higher... Wherever you touch our education system, major deficiencies undermining the future of children and country emerge.

How prominently does FE figure in such deliberations? Do those who seek to improve the nation's education and training see FE as having a central role to play? or as responsible for alleged deficiencies?

Government interest in FE

I looked first at **Education**, a weekly publication that provides regular reports on any educational matters debated in Parliament. In the 104 issues from July 1988 to July 1990 (Volumes 172-5) there were 524 reports of Parliamentary discussions involving education. Of these 52 per cent (273) concerned schools, 31 per cent (161) matters of general educational interest not related to any specific sector, 15 per cent (78) HE, and two per cent (12) FE. One would have to conclude that on those occasions when Parliament discusses education, FE is a subject of only very minor interest and political importance or – an interesting thought – a sector in which everything is going wonderfully well, for which reason there is little to debate.

Another area of activity that could reveal some indication of interest is the publications list of HMSO. What government chooses to print helps to form debating agendas and provides some suggestion of relative importance as seen from the centre. In the period covering 1988, 1989 and the first half of 1990, of a total of 182 HMSO publications on education 43 per cent (79) were concerned with general issues, 29 per cent (52) with schools, 19 per cent (35) with HE and nine per cent (16) with FE.

One is forced to conclude that even if it accommodates 30 per cent of all members of the UK population involved in public-sector education and 74 per cent of those above school-leaving age similarly occupied, FE is not an area in which central government exhibits a conspicuous amount of interest. FE is of only limited political importance. It does not appear to dominate the thoughts of Members of Parliament. In the DES, the major focus of concern seems to skirt around rather than focus on FE.

It is not that government has no interest in training, the area in which FE holds public sector hegemony. During the past decade we have been repeatedly reminded of how badly trained our population is compared to those of competitor countries. Among 16 to 18 year olds, for example, only 35 per cent were in full-time education or training in 1988, while Australia, Belgium, Canada, Denmark, France, Germany, Italy, Japan, the Netherlands, Spain, Sweden and the United States had participation rates of between 47 per cent and 77 per cent (DES, 1990).

Despite such concern, government has tended to regard training as an activity with problems that can best be solved through the agency of employers rather than the efforts of individual employees. Indeed, training as presented by the Employment Department appears to be primarily an employer issue, even though research indicates that many employees train not to assist their current bosses but to leave the present firm for a better job (Theodossin and Thomson, 1987). In **Training for jobs** (DE/DES, 1984) colleges were castigated not for failing their students (except indirectly) but for providing training which did not meet employer needs.

The dominance of employers in the training field has been further strengthened by three other events. The 1988 Education Reform Act in England and Wales and Part II of the Self-Governing Schools etc. (Scotland) Act of 1989 effectively reduced the size of college governing bodies (making them more like executive boards) and required not fewer than half of the body to be drawn from employment interest groups and co-optees.

When the Government established the Training Commission (TC) in June 1988 it increased the number of Commissioners to include more employer representatives. This changed the balance among employers, trades unionists and local government and education commissioners. The Trades Union Congress subsequently withdrew support for the Employment Training programme, in response to which the Government in September of the same year announced that the TC would be replaced by the Training Agency.

This effectively got rid of the tripartite arrangements which had existed in Britain during the post-war period and which are still present in most Western European countries. As Hall (1990) puts it, 'The right of employees and their trades unions to act as equal social partners with employers has been scrapped in place of direct control by employers'.

In addition, the establishment of Training and Enterprise Councils (TECs) in England and Wales and Local Enterprise Companies (LECs) in Scotland links the planning and delivery of training (contracted with government) to the development of small businesses and self-employment. TECs and LECs will manage training programmes for young people, for unemployed people, and for adults requiring new knowledge and technical retraining. Many of the TECs have been based on local Chambers of Commerce, the Confederation of British Industry or Local Employer Networks – all bringing industry more centrally into training provision.

Nor has government been inclined to view colleges as either the only or necessarily the best provider of training. In the 1980s training became a market-place activity competed for by private sector providers and public sector colleges. Upon occasion, colleges crossed the boundary to overcome what they saw as an innate disadvantage (Spink, 1988).

> I don't know if this was a nation-wide policy, but certainly in south-east Surrey the MSC was reluctant to allow FE colleges to become managing agents for YTS. My then principal and I decided that the only way to get around this was to form an external body. This would be a college company, totally independent from the college but set up for its benefit, feeding work into the college and giving young people a good training. This was our rationale for setting up the company, not making money.

Policy or not, what Spink describes is a world in which government has openly stimulated the private sector to compete with the public sector.

The 1988 Education Reform Act pushed colleges further towards the business model, imposing on them the kinds of commercial considerations which are taken for granted in the market-place and depriving them of the certainties – and excuses for any failure to deliver – which the local authority once provided. One interesting and revealing feature of the debate surrounding the 1988 Act was how completely it centred on schools and how persistently FE was ignored. In the past decade, the Government's determined efforts to dismantle protectionist arrangements in the professions – e.g. banking, law, medicine, education – have proved particularly successful in FE.

This trend continues, as is clearly revealed in the FE White Paper (DES, 1991). At first glance, the Paper might be viewed as evidence of Government support for FE: the DES must have begun to take CFEs seriously for such a document to be produced at all. Upon reflection, however, doubts emerge. Few of the details needed to translate grand designs into practical arrangements are present, while the Paper has been used as a vehicle for a number of proposals which are unlikely to benefit FE at all.

We are told that by the autumn of 1991 Youth Training will be directed 'entirely by TECs and LECs' – the inevitable end to a decade-long effort to shift control of training to employers. Schools will be allowed to recruit adults as fee-paying students and vocational education is to be promoted in schools as one means of bridging the academic-vocational divide. The Government also intends to introduce a single school-leaving date at the end of the summer term, to encourage pupils 'to complete their studies...and to have their achievements assessed', but also as a means of reducing pressure for jobs without incurring additional expenses. All of these proposed changes must inevitably increase competition for both school leavers and adults.

So, too, must the Government's aim

> ...to offer every 16 and 17 year old leaving full-time education a training credit within the lifetime of the next Parliament.

The scheme involves a credit or voucher worth between £1,500 and £2,000 which will enable the holder to buy training from specialists, employers or colleges (Guardian, 31 August 1990) – and, provided TECs offer them accreditation, schools as well. To speed up the operation, the Government's commitment to training credits has pre-dated the published findings of the pilot studies begun in April 1991 in 11 TECs and LECs.

Employers and colleges can now expect to compete openly for what may be lucrative individual training contracts, as money which was previously spent on students via the local college is channelled through the customers to the trainers of their choice. Such an arrangement could well provide employers with the kind of stimulus to train which government efforts have so far failed to deliver. CFEs may still be the major vocational trainers on a head count, but their hegemony will need to be defended. Central government would claim that the proposed incorporation of FE colleges is the best means of enabling CFEs to do battle for business successfully. Whether that is so only time will reveal.

At local government level the position of FE is – and has always been – no less peripheral than at central level. Many local authority education departments are responsible for dozens of primary and secondary schools but in many instances only one college, or when there are two or more a tendency to reduce the number. Reorganising schools, whether through amalgamation or closure, can be relied upon to arouse parental wrath because it is seen as disrupting children's education. Protest campaigns can be expected. In many authorities, attempts to produce a comprehensive tertiary system have been successfully challenged by school lobbying. By contrast, FE college reorganisation on its own usually goes unnoticed outside staff rooms. Politically – centrally and locally – colleges occupy a tangential position.

Despite that position, the White Paper proposals to remove CFEs entirely from LEA control has aroused oppostion in some quarters. The press have reported rumblings from infuriated Tory councillors (Nash, 1991). Other reports (Education, 1991), however, suggest that if Labour were returned to power it would not oppose incorporation, but that LEAs, along with TECs, would be 'responsible for strategic planning', a modification, but hardly a wholesale rejection. Unlike school education and the National Health Service, FE does not appear to be a territory over which major political parties are interested in doing battle.

FE and the national press

Government preoccupation as revealed in activity, debate and publications is only one potential index of public interest. Three so-called 'quality' newspapers now devote part of a weekly issue to discussing education: The Guardian, The Independent and The Times. The four-week period from 14 May to 4 June 1990 traditionally covers the last time in the English and Welsh academic session when teaching staff can hand in their notices and still be replaced before the following year (31 May is the legal closing date for resigning before the end of the summer term). It is therefore a time when schools and colleges advertise fairly extensively in the hope of recruiting staff for September. It is also a period in which educational institutions (although not necessarily FE) are still advertising for autumn enrolments.

Table 5 provides an analysis of the three 'qualities' over this period in square centimetres of how much space was devoted to advertising on the one hand and news reporting and feature writing (hitherto referred to as 'coverage') on the other. Collectively, schools account for only eight per cent of the advertising but receive 67 per cent of the coverage. By way of contrast, HE pays for 50 per cent of the advertising but receives only 14 per cent of the coverage. Independent FE provides 1.5 per cent of the advertising but receives three per cent of the coverage, while maintained FE achieves precisely the reverse: three per cent of the advertising and 1.5 per cent of the coverage.

Table 5 Analysis by square centimetres of educational advertising and news/features in the weekly education sections of three quality newspapers during the weeks of 14, 21, 28 May and 4 June 1990.

Newspaper	Advertising in cm^2					News/features in cm^2				
	Maintained	Independent	Schools	HE	Other	Maintained	Independent	Schools	HE	Other
Guardian	5,966	1,832	11,967	99,274	83,588	669	—	21,578	1,120	5,507
% total advertising (202,627 cm^2)	3%	1%	6%	49%	41%					
% of total news etc. (28,874cm^2)						2%		75%	4%	19%
Independent	885	543	3,088	12,349	453	—	700	2,614	4,289	15
% total advertising (17,318cm^2)	5%	3%	18%	71%	3%					
% of total news etc. (7,618 cm^2)						—	9%	34%	56%	—
Times	104	1,084	3,696	4,230	921	16	622	5,084	948	978
% total advertising (10,035 cm^2)	1%	11%	37%	42%	9%					
% of total news etc. (8,408 cm^2)						—	8%	69%	11%	12%
Overall percentage advertising or news etc.	3%	1.5%	8%	50%	37%	1.5%	3%	67%	14%	14%

Newspapers are, of course, not obliged to produce coverage proportional to advertising volume, although it is not uncommon for the press to feature particular areas of activity which attract related advertising (the Independent of 17 May spotlit independent FE in its education section, with substantial advertising from this sector during this and the subsequent week). Maintained FE, however, is clearly regarded as of only limited interest to either the general public or anyone reading FE advertising.

Since the so-called 'popular' press treats all of education as an area of limited concern, and even the 'quality' press regularly providing education coverage demonstrates only tangential interest in FE, one may be right in concluding that either the public considers FE as inconsequential or – because news is largely a man-made construct – no one has yet stimulated its interest. The result is a kind of unending circle: because the general public hears nothing about FE it has no interest in FE, which explains why the general public hears nothing about FE...

And what of the specialist educational press? During the same four-week period noted above, The Times Higher Education Supplement (THES) devoted 1.7 per cent of its coverage to FE topics, a proportion comparable to that to be found in the quality press. HE's interest in FE derives from the fact that it recruits some of its students from FE (via A level and Access courses).

However, where one might expect to find much more substantial coverage of FE is in The Times Educational Supplement (TES) which ostensibly offers news and features on everything from nursery to higher education, with the latter given only limited cover since it has its own sister weekly. **Table 6** sets out an analysis by square centimetres of advertising and coverage in the same four-week period. Here the results are surprising. Schools provide 54 per cent of the advertising and get 69 per cent of the coverage; HE one per cent of each of the advertising and the coverage; and FE six per cent of the advertising and 1.6 per cent of the coverage, a smaller proportion than in the THES.

There is another point to consider. Much of the coverage referred to in the above analyses is about FE in only the very broadest sense, i.e. about post-compulsory training outside schools. Thus one is less likely to read about CFEs as such than about: drop-outs (Maclure, 1990, Jackson, 1990) who prefer immediate money to investment in training; TECs and the opportunities they represent (Cridland, 1990, Tytler, 1990); or changes in post-16 education in Lewisham (Hilton, 1990). Not only is FE treated as an inconsequential general subject, but when it is mentioned in any feature it is often regarded as peripheral to the subject under discussion.

Table 6 Analysis by square centimetres of educational advertising and news/features in the Times Educational Supplement, 11, 18, 25 May and 1 June 1990.

Subject	Advertising		News/features	
	cm^2	Per cent	cm^2	Per cent
FE	28,858	6.3	2,420	1.6
Schools	314,994	68.6	84,190	54.3
HE	4,725	1.0	1,637	1.0
Other	110,503	24.1	66,880	43.1
Total	459,080	100	155,127	100

One can see the indifference most clearly with regard to the subject variously known as LMS (local management of schools) or LMC (local management of colleges): the devolution of financial autonomy to public sector educational establishments. As a consequence of the 1988 Education Reform Act, since 1 April 1990 schools and colleges in England and Wales (Scotland followed in October 1990) have been concerned to manage their financial affairs in very much more of the style and approach usually associated with business.

In its issues from 18 May to 16 June 1990, the TES ran 13 items on LMS, one a double-page feature (18 May) and three other major articles. There was nothing on LMC, even though up and down the country hundreds (but obviously not thousands) of colleges were facing similar problems.

The TES is not the only source of information about education. To check out the situation elsewhere, in July 1990 I selected 25 journals taken by The Staff College library and examined their contents over the previous two years. These were publications either about education generally (Journal of Curriculum Studies) but not specifically devoted to FE, or journals which might from time to time be expected to print a paper on education (British Journal of Sociology). Only articles were considered. The survey was not absolutely comprehensive: some issues were missing. It nonetheless offered a general overview of FE's position in a broader range of publications.

Table 7 sets out the findings. Only two journals had nothing in them about education. Most of the printed material (85 per cent) was not about a particular educational sector. Among all the published papers, nine per cent were about schools, four per cent about HE and two per cent about FE. To some extent this must be FE's fault, for many, if not all, of the journals depend on unsolicited contributions: if FE wants to be read about more often, its teachers and researchers will have to produce more papers. It is difficult to escape the conclusion that FE maintains a very low profile in the educational world: in terms of press and journal coverage, two per cent and less is not a substantial proportion.

FE incorporation and the national press

The above draws upon material which predates the announcement that CFEs were to be taken from LEA control (21 March 1991) and the ensuing FE White Paper (DES, 1991). If ever there was a time when FE could expect maximum national coverage, surely this was it.

The proposed changes did indeed bring FE into the picture even if not into what one might call central focus. On the day following the March House of Commons revelation of impending CFE incorporation, the quality press carried the news, even if as something of a footnote to the lead story, the replacement of the community charge/poll tax.

The Times (Tytler, 1991) and The Independent (MacLeod, 1991a) ran front page stories about the removal of FE colleges from LEA control, while The Guardian (Bates and Meikle, 1991) gave details on an inside page. The latter compensated by mentioning FE in its leader – even if only to view its proposed incorporation as evidence of 'the long unhappy trend towards tighter and tighter control from the centre' – while the Times and Independent ran leaders which managed to avoid mentioning CFEs altogether.

The TES, going to bed before the Commons announcement, emerged on the next day without any notice of the big FE story. It did, however, suggest that something similar had been rumoured. A Platform article (Morris, 1991) warned against using education as a 'quick fix over [the] poll tax' and a leader (TES, 1991a) entitled 'Steal the schools to get out of a poll-tax problem' reiterated the warning.

The following week, upon reflection, the TES chose not to lead with the FE story (stale by this time). Instead, it provided a page three account (Jackson, 1991a) and an equivocal FE leader (TES, 1991b) which rehearsed points for and against incorporation, concluding that many questions remain to be answered. Somewhat

Table 7   Analysis of content of subject matter of main articles in a variety of journals

Publication	No.	Dates	Schools	FE	HE	Other	Total
Adults Learning	8	1989-90	0	7	5	52	64
British Journal of Ed. Technology	6	1988-90	3	0	0	31	34
British Journal of Guidance & Counselling	7	1988-90	1	3	1	51	56
British Journal of Sociology	6	1989-90	0	0	1	44	45
Bulletin of Teaching and Learning	3	1988-90	0	0	5	33	38
County Councils Gazette	18	1988-90	1	0	0	143	144
Educational Change and Development	6	1988-90	10	0	3	11	24
Educational Management and Administration	4	1989	15	2	1	15	33
Educational Research	5	1989-90	10	0	0	32	42
Journal of Curriculum Studies	9	1989-90	8	0	0	27	35
Journal of Educational Policy	6	1989-90	7	1	1	21	30
Journal of Educational Administration & History	5	1988-90	2	1	0	29	32
Journal of Education for Teaching	5	1989-90	8	0	2	15	25
Journal of Management Studies	9	1989-90	1	0	0	48	49
Learning Resources Journal	4	1989-90	0	2	1	18	21
Local Government Policy Making	6	1989-90	1	1	0	48	50
Local Government Studies	7	1989-90	0	0	0	44	44
Management in Education	6	1989-90	10	3	3	29	45
Oxford Review of Education	6	1988-89	0	0	2	49	51
Research in Education	5	1988-90	6	0	1	32	39
Research Papers in Education	5	1988-90	5	0	7	27	39
Scottish Educational Review	5	1988-90	6	0	1	27	34
Teaching News (B'ham)	7	1988-90	0	0	5	13	18
Welsh Journal of Education	2	1989-90	2	0	0	10	12
Women in Management Review	6	1989-90	0	0	0	16	16
Totals	156		96	20	39	865	1,020
Percentage of totals			9	2	4	85	100

more positively, the THES (Tysome, 1991a) devoted nearly half of page two to the FE news. In a later issue, a TES Platform article by a chief education officer (Collier, 1991) mourned 'the removal of colleges from local education authority control'. The earth did not move and the heavens did not cleave, but FE had had its day.

Understandably, the subsequent FE White Paper caused less excitement, although an unusual feature of this document is the number of important proposals it makes about schools – a single leaving date, an altered academic culture, recruitment of adults, etc. – which appear to have attracted far less notice than they might have if they had been included in a document devoted primarily to schools.

Sandwiched between the Commons incorporation announcment and the White Paper was the formal launching of the FE Marketing Unit on 15 April 1991. This was an important FE occasion, graced by the Secretary of State for Education and Science as leading speaker and, some three weeks after the incorporation announcement, an event at which FE might legitimately expect to make the news headlines.

Journalists from appropriate national newspapers were invited and most, according to organisers' reports, came, listened and lunched. On the following day, however, the education story which made news was the announcement from the junior minister, Michael Fallon, that schools in England would be required to publish truancy figures from the following year (MacLeod, 1991b). By a stroke of irony, the one national paper which did report the Unit's opening and record Mr Clarke's presence, the THES, inadvertently mistook the FE Marketing Unit for the 'Further Education Marketing Network'. The Network is, of course, quite distinct from the Unit, and represents not just FE but HE as well.

If FE's activities do not often appear to be quite the news that those who work in it might hope, there is always the possibility that it is not that FE is ignored so much as that it is not very interesting. Journalists do not often overlook exciting leads. One FE event which seemed to attract a substantial share of national press coverage was the financial collapse of Coventry Technical College (a reported loss of £5.5m, four resignations, scores of redundancies, etc.). On 3 May 1991 this inspired both a TES story (Jackson, 1991b) and a leader. Nearly three months later an even more extensive article (MacLeod, 1991c) surfaced in the Independent. Making the news is not always a comfortable experience.

FE and other national media

FE is even less likely to be encountered on television or radio than in the national press. Few news or discussion programmes touch on FE except in reference to training, at which time the point at issue is seldom likely to be delivery venue. Unlike polytechnic and university lecturers, FE staff do not appear regularly to comment as experts on aspects of professional activity. FE has had no major TV series centred on its precincts as have schools (Grange Hill) and universities (The History Man).

In the middle of 1991, the BBC announced two series for transmission in the latter part of 1991 and the first half of 1992. Both are responses to a familiar problem expounded in the promotional brochure.

> The British economy faces intractable problems because of its under-educated, under-trained and under-qualified workforce. It is now being widely recognised that there is an urgent need to develop a learning culture radically different from that of the present.
>
> Educational broadcasting is well placed to make a substantial contribution to this development. The innovative **Second chance** and **The training hour** initiatives from BBC Education aim to encourage individuals to return to learning and to take up education and training opportunities which will both transform their lives and contribute positively to the economic and social well being of the nation.

Prior to viewing the actual programmes, one cannot evaluate FE's role. CFEs figure in the promotional material, but only peripherally. Among the 61 'external attendees' at the **Second chance** reception on 1 July 1991, only eight (13 per cent) could be said to represent FE. From among them, only four (seven per cent) came from FE colleges, and only three colleges sent attendees. The sole FE professional organisation attending was NATFHE (which also serves HE).

In the literature for the **Second chance** series, it is suggested that 'FE colleges and adult education centres' will be promoting adult education and training 'at local and regional level' during the week of 9 to 15 March 1992. Colleges are also to figure – along with Adult Guidance Services, the Careers Service, the Employment Service, the Department of Social Security, TECs, Citizens Advice Bureaux, Enterprise Agencies and voluntary bodies – in the provision of a national free telephone advice service. FE is clearly present, possibly only just visible in the crowd, but unmistakably there. Its size, scope and market share might, however, suggest that more than presence is appropriate.

Such treatment is hardly the fault of television producers. The world does not owe FE – or any providing agency – extensive and regular exposure, sympathetic treatment and deep understanding. A national service seeking to promote itself has first to identify the image it wishes to promulgate. After that it has but a single feasible line of action, to invest its own resources – time, energy, talent, money – in the desired perceptual transformation. In the market-place, dominant images and high profiles are made, not born.

If FE deserves the epithets which its own staff have used to describe how the world views CFEs – peripheral, a very grey area, a mystery – FE is itself largely at fault. We need to examine why this is the case.

Chapter 5:
The FE sub-culture

Like most groups which are marginalised in collective social activity, FE has sought to protect itself by creating its own sub-culture. In many respects it has been better provided for than higher profile sectors, even if they gain more media coverage and figure centrally in public debate. Although many may ignore it, FE more than compensates by looking after its own interests very effectively.

To start with, FE has access to a large range of publications devoted to issues of professional interest to college staff. Bulletins and news-sheets are published regularly by examining bodies such as the Business and Technology Education Council, the City and Guilds of London Institute, the National Examining Board for Supervisory Management, and the Scottish Vocational Education Council. The Employment Department through its Training Agency, has produced a string of regular publications (e.g. **Employment Training News, Insight, Tourism and Training Newsletter**).

Specialist journals related to areas of FE activity are put out by organisations such as the National Institute of Adult Continuing Education, the Adult Literacy and Basic Skills Unit, and Guildford Education Services. Linked with HE are the **Journal for Further and Higher Education in Scotland** and the **Journal of Further and Higher Education** (for the rest of the UK), the **National Association for Staff Development in Further and Higher Education Journal** and the **Coombe Lodge Reports**. On the international scene FE is served by the European Centre for the Development of Vocational Training and the European Information Network on Local Employment Initiatives, as well as by a wide variety of American journals (many devoted to community colleges).

FE staff seeking to read about their organisations and their curriculum areas cannot thus be described as deprived. National newspapers and journals may ignore it most of the time, but FE has an extensive range of periodicals to keep it abreast of its own and comparable international developments.

Moreover, in the 1980s, the Government's attitude to FE was not without its more generous aspect. Alongside the criticism of CFEs and the stimulation and apparent favouring of private sector competition, substantial national resources were directed towards FE, largely on the grounds that criticism ought to be accompanied by financial support, so that FE could put its house in order. One might argue that the Government was actually taking away more with one hand that it was giving back with the other, that the MSC and TA funds which came to FE were extracted from FE's own funding and used to promote areas of Government concern, but it ought to be recalled that many public sector activities endured comparable resource cuts without significant reinvestment of what was withdrawn.

FE has not failed to reap some benefits from Government preoccupation with training in recent years. It has been funded for a vast range of college, LEA and national projects, as well as benefiting financially from various youth training programmes. In the early 1980s MSC money was frequently used to upgrade college equipment and bring in new technology. Work on a computerised national FE directory was undertaken by the Educational Counselling and Credit Transfer Information Service (now privatised) and the TA's Training Access Points. For much of the decade the Government also helped fund the Further Education Management Information System project, which developed computer software for college resource management.

One obvious benefit was the Responsive College Programme (RCP), run by the Further Education Staff College and funded (£2.25m) by the MSC/TA. From the beginning of 1986 to the end of 1988, working in English, Scottish and Welsh local authorities, RCP ran 10 two-year projects (Bedfordshire, Birmingham, Cleveland, Doncaster, Gwynedd, Lancashire, Lincolnshire, Newham, Sheffield, and Strathclyde) and 11 one-year projects (Buckinghamshire, Calderdale, Dudley, Dyfed, East Sussex, Hereford and Worcester, Kent, Salford, Somerset, Suffolk and West Glamorgan).

Over 50 full-time staff were employed in RCP and the results of their work were published (Theodossin, 1989b) in a large package with a book, two manuals (one for marketeers, the other for senior managers), three videos, training slides, and a vast array of illustrative examples which involved actors, models, graphic designers, copywriters, photographers and illustrators. The publication was launched in London, Belfast, Cardiff and Edinburgh with the help of Government ministers. The military may be accustomed to expenditure on a grander scale, but in the world of education, project funding has usually been measured in tens of thousands of pounds rather than millions. Again, nothing comparable was done for schools or HE.

Although it is not statutory for either FE or HE teachers to be trained, FE (but not HE) has its own specialist teacher training provision located in four centres in England (Bolton, London, Huddersfield and Wolverhampton). Other, more general training is also provided by a number of polytechnics. In Scotland, the School of Further Education based at Jordanhill College of Education trains FE teachers.

FE also has the Further Education Unit (FEU), a curriculum body, initiated in 1977, which has run more than 400 projects in the past 13 years. It is funded by the DES, although in 1983 it was made a limited company. The FEU has few educational rivals in the distribution of printed material. Its 1986-89 catalogue lists 175 publications, all available free of charge and ranging in length from two to 284 pages. In addition there are 28 entries for priced publications, from £3.75 to £55.00. The extent to which so large a production volume is genuinely beneficial is sometimes debated, but FE teaching staff cannot claim that their curriculum interests and needs are being ignored.

Nothing comparable to the FEU – apart from a recently established Scottish version – can currently be found anywhere in UK education. One needs to look back to the 1960s and '70s and the Schools Council for so large a national organisation similarly devoted to producing material by and for teachers, and most of the Schools Council's products were sold rather than distributed free of charge. Like the Schools Council, the FEU has from time to time aroused government antagonism, but unlike it, the FEU has so far survived. The extent and variety of FEU preoccupations are wide and diverse: moral competence, entrepreneurial skills, foreign language learning for business and industry, gender and multicultural issues, distribution education, interactive video, staff development, etc. - and all related directly to FE.

FE also has The Staff College (formerly Coombe Lodge, more recently The Further Education Staff College) which provides specialist management training for FE staff (and to a lesser extent public sector HE staff). The Staff College was founded in 1963 as an independent charitable trust and considerably expanded in the second half of the 1980s. It generates the bulk of its income through the sale of goods and services but also receives grants from LEAs in England and Wales, the Scottish local authorities and the Department of Education, Northern Ireland.

The Staff College offers both central (in Blagdon, near Bristol) and UK regional training events for college managers. It produces a journal (**Coombe Lodge Reports**, noted above) and runs a publications department (this book is one of its titles), which offers books, papers and training materials for LEA and college staff and college governors. The Staff College also delivers commissioned customised training and consultancy services. Recently it has developed a diploma programme and is currently establishing an MBA. The Staff College is unique: no other education staff college exists (or has ever existed) for any other UK education sector.

The size of the FE market has traditionally discouraged private-sector publishers from including FE on their lists: a mailing to 500 colleges does not look impressive beside a comparable one to 29,000 schools. During the past decade both FEU and The Staff College have, therefore, been able to corner what is a relatively small market and to build up a body of highly specialised professional literature. More recently, with the introduction of desktop publishing, colleges and LEAs have also begun to enter the publishing field, making the work of their own FE teachers available to colleagues across the country. In earlier years FE lecturers attending award-bearing HE courses found themselves in a minority among school teachers and were faced with extrapolating what they could from published work centred on other areas of the education service. FE staff are still likely to belong to a minority, but their reading interests are increasingly well served.

Inevitably, neither the FEU nor The Staff College is widely known among the majority of teachers outside FE. The FEU's work has sometimes won appreciation in sixth-form colleges, and The Staff College is familiar to some public-sector HE managers, but both organisations are primarily part of the FE sub-culture.

If one were seeking a prototype of that sub-culture one need look no further than immigrant ethnic minority groups in Britain. Many such Asian groups, for example, recreate something of their own cultures in the midst of quite different British life. They build temples to worship in, establish schools for their children's education, publish their own newspapers, provide films for their own cinemas, run their own specialist food and clothing shops for the distribution of imported goods, and congregate together in a continuing programme of social activities. FE resembles these groups in many respects.

Outsiders are generally unaware of the services and support structures the FE sub-culture has established for itself. When they wander into the distinctive world of FE, they are often genuinely startled to discover a curriculum agency devoted exclusively to the production of materials for a relatively small part of the education service, or a management training centre located in the midst of some of the most beautiful countryside in south-west England and housing an extensive specialist library. A marginal sub-culture need not be a materially deprived sub-culture.

Compensating for insecurities

Despite any material advantages they may possess, under the well resourced surface many sub-culture members are insecure. One way of dealing with the consequences is to emphasise the distinctiveness of the sub-culture, and the most effective way of doing so is through language. Like many such groups, FE has its own coded language which is constantly being expanded by members. The result is not a language with its own syntax or grammar, but one which is characterised by a plethora of initialisms and acronyms. Thus, in FE-speak one can say or write,

> The ALH must be raised and the ASH cut if we're going to improve the SSR. If we don't do this, we're going to find it difficult to introduce new NVQ and NEBSS work.

This generates a need for a glossary of acronyms and initialisms. The Staff College publishes and regularly updates a document on 'essential' initialisms and acronyms which at last count had passed the 400 mark (Graystone, 1991). Such language is also generated in other sub-group cultures, but FE seems to require the security of its own language more desperately than other groups and consequently seems to create more esoteric vocabulary on a weekly basis than any of its competitors. The alleged purpose is to speed up communication, but the volume of paper which FE produces about itself suggests brevity is not a genuine consideration. Rather, esoteric language is a form of protection: it separates those who belong from those who do not. When people fail to communicate, the most frequent reason is that they do not wish to do so.

One result is that outsiders such as employers find FE baffling. People who talk to one another about PBOG, PEL, PETRA, PICKUP, PIN, PRC and PRE can expect little beyond bewilderment from anyone who overhears them. This can be advantageous, particularly with main culture members (e.g. governors and employers) who might otherwise imagine they understood what was and was not going on in the college.

Members of sub-cultures often have deep-rooted doubts about their own worth and suffer from low self-esteem. To those who live and work in the main culture, the dimly perceived and little understood sub-culture can appear sub-standard, which in turn can lead to unflattering stereotyping. Such external attitudes – while often strenuously opposed and denied in public – can come to seem privately valid within the sub-culture. It often takes considerable determination and self-confidence for sub-culture members not to be demoralised.

Feelings of inherent inadequacy surface in FE most noticeably in the difficulty it experiences in presenting itself – or sometimes even thinking of itself – as providing something which is intrinsically valuable. Hence the favourite FE self-image as a venue for access to HE, i.e. as a doorway through which one passes from an unsatisfactory experience to a better one, but like all doorways of no real interest in itself – rather like regarding France primarily as a gateway to Germany or Italy, instead of as a country whose people and culture are worth cultivating for their own sakes. In the feasibility study, two respondents put this view very succinctly.

> We are the place to go to. We link to HE... (Vice-principal)

> Those who know about FE think it's very important. It gives access to HE. (Principal)

Another popular image within FE is of colleges as purveyors of second chances, i.e. opportunities to overcome failure elsewhere.

> Most people think of FE as a college which provides an opportunity for a second chance at all ages. (Principal)

> The 16+ market sees us as the vocational route, a second chance, an alternative to school (especially if they don't like it). (College marketing officer)

Underlying the idea of a 'second chance' is the notion of human life needing to conform to a stereotypical pattern. Anyone who fails to achieve the requisite qualifications at the preordained time has wasted a first chance. The very concept of a 'second chance' thus forms what one might describe as a defeatist charter, carrying overtones of disapprobation and failure, of lawbreaking and misdemeanours. With potential students it is patronising.

Like most educational establishments of relatively low status, FE is an agency of conservatism and of conformity to transmitted social values. In FE colleges the staff most likely to be appointed to senior positions are those with academic rather than vocational backgrounds. How many college principals have hairdressing or catering backgrounds?

The British social class system with its gradations of status is still reflected at all levels in the average FE college, not least in the divisions between academic and support staff (until recently known pejoratively as non-teaching staff). Not only do the two groups work under strikingly different conditions of service and pay scales, but in most colleges they are divided socially and have different staff rooms and different dining arrangements. There are also comparable social class distinctions to be noted among curriculum areas, among staff and students, and among student groups. Anyone seeking a classless society would be hard pressed to locate it in FE.

FE is frequently its own worst enemy. So long as many of those in CFEs – staff and students – view themselves as there because they failed to get in somewhere else, it remains difficult for FE to regard and to present itself positively. The tattiness of FE buildings and the unfriendly reception areas can be (and often are) blamed on resource constraints, but they are also the natural consequence of low self-esteem.

Thus at the heart of the FE sub-culture lies the ambivalence of the marginalised minority group, with fierce pride in its distinctiveness coupled with private feelings of inadequacy. The uncertainty often comes across as negative. As one respondent put it.

> It's confused. There's no clear picture of how FE relates. It the catch-all. It's where you go if you can't find anywhere else. It's not a positive image offering anything particular. In inner cities it's a second chance. (Principal)

Conversely, belonging to a sub-culture can also offer distinct advantages to members. For example, much of the publicity which attaches to schools centres on alleged deficiencies in the school system, the ways in which primary and secondary teachers are sometimes believed to be failing the youth of the nation. While it may still be exposed to government strictures, FE's lower profile at least spares its lecturers the acrimony of dealing with openly voiced disapproval from the general public. Letter writers to the BBC and national newspapers seldom touch on FE.

There is also another aspect of FE organisation which sets it advantageously apart from other educational sectors: for many years FE academic staff have enjoyed clearly defined conditions of service which establish precisely what teachers can and cannot be required to do. For each graded salary scale there have been minimum and maximum contact hours decreasing as the lecturer rises in status, so that senior staff are paid more to teach less. There have been remission and abatement arrangements for additional duties, restrictions as to how many evenings and how many hours per day a lecturer can be timetabled to teach. There has been no tradition of covering for colleagues without payment or of unpaid self-sacrifice for the good of the service: overtime pay has been needed to reimburse lecturers who work above their maximum workload, if they agree to do so. Nor are staff contractually required to remain on college premises when they are not teaching. The FE remuneration ethic clearly derives from the business world from which many lecturers have come.

School teachers have never enjoyed anything comparable: the loss of free periods to cover for absent colleagues has been the norm. The school day has never been defined in terms of anything other than a minimum number of hours. Hence schools start and finish at various times and workload is measured in 'periods' whose length can vary from school to school.

FE conditions of service have been the source of considerable envy among those teachers who work under less well defined arrangements and who are aware of FE's advantages. When in the formation of tertiary colleges, staff (depending on their origins) have been employed on both teacher and FE conditions of service, quite justifiable resentment has resulted.

In recent years, with the Education Reform Act and a move towards plant bargaining, many of the constraints have come under fire and one can expect pressure for greater flexibility in the future. Here, too, however, FE can be said to have benefited from its relative isolation. The Audit Commission's (1985) potentially sensational findings (high levels of remission, underemployment and overpayment of staff, etc.) caused far less professional embarrassment than they might have done had they concerned school teachers. FE has usually managed to look after its own interests more effectively than have teachers in other sectors. Invisibility can occasionally confer benefits.

Sub-groups in the sub-culture

There are, on the other hand, distinct disadvantages to membership of a relatively obscure sub-culture. In an interesting and useful analogy, Hall (1990) describes FE's isolation as an enclave, i.e. a country in the middle of a land mass bounded by foreign dominions, of which the prime example is Poland where,

> ...higher education is the Russian Bear to the east and the school system is the German Eagle to the west. To the south are the various types of training organisations that have come and gone in the post-war period. All of them compete to some extent with further education and there are overlaps of student populations. In the post-war period, further education has succeeded in pushing back the boundaries as it has expanded.

In recent years, with a smaller youth market, FE has been facing further boundary incursions from its neighbours: HE, schools, TECs, private trainers, etc. Such a position is unlikely to be comfortable. Hall notes that

> The major difficulty for a small country sandwiched between large empires is that those neighbours can use their strength to push back the frontiers at any time, unless they are prevented by hostile public opinion.

Public opinion, in turn, is unlikely to be aroused by low profile distress or anxiety. More than in the past, FE needs to promote itself and to raise public awareness of its existence, usefulness and value. As educational competition increases, invisibility is less and less an advantage.

FE has distinct difficulties in drawing attention to itself at the national level. To some extent the FE features described above are necessarily true only of England and Wales. Scotland has its own arrangements – even though its colleges resemble their English and Welsh counterparts more than its schools do – which brings us to another important feature of FE provision, the abundance of agencies which can be said to represent CFEs.

If one thinks in terms of lecturers, there are the National Association of Teachers in Further and Higher Education (NATFHE) and the Educational Institute of Scotland. Support staff – potentially capable of growing at the expense of teaching staff as resource constraints impinge – are represented by the National and Local Government Officers Association (NALGO). If one is seeking a spokesperson for college management, one might go to the Association of Principals of Colleges, the Association of Vice-Principals of Colleges, the Association of Colleges for Further and Higher Education, the Association of College Registrars and Administrators, or the Association for College Management – or, possibly, the National Association of Governors and Managers, the Association of Metropolitan Authorities, the Association of County Councils, the Council of Local Education Authorities, all of whom still (until incorporation) have something to do with managing colleges. The above lists are by no means exhaustive. The sub-culture may look relatively homogeneous from a distance, but from close up the splits and conflicts of interest among various sub-groups are only too evident.

The national newspaper advertising campaign run by the National Union of Teachers in autumn 1990 to lobby for increased resources for schools is precisely the sort of activity which has thus far proved beyond the capability of FE. FE's major teachers' union – NATFHE – lacks the resources for campaigning on a similar scale.

Nor would it be easy for FE's chief executives, the college principals, to organise themselves into something like the Committee of Directors of Polytechnics and produce anything comparable to the polytechnics' 1988 prospectus, **Services to industry and commerce**. This full-colour, highly professional publication promoted polytechnic services to employers, had a foreword by The Prince of Wales and was sponsored by British Gas, Hydro Energy Associates, IBM and WH Smith. FE principals have never managed to organise themselves sufficiently to undertake anything so adventurous. Numbers may be one reason (there are many more CFEs than polytechnics), but divisiveness is probably another. As we have seen, there is not one managerial association, or even one major such association, but an assortment of groups reflecting many and varied distinctions and differences.

The divisions in FE are deep. Like so much of education, FE has its infinite graduations of rank and political clout which account for the diverse agencies. Because they represent conflicting interests and distinctions within the college world, no one agency can be said to represent FE to the wider world. An editor looking for comment on a current news item could expect quite different responses from different agencies, and should any one attempt to claim hegemony, the remainder would be sure to protest.

Unlike the Confederation of British Industry, which regularly commissions surveys of its members and publishes warnings and predictions which are taken up by the press, FE's agencies attempt nothing so ambitious. Nor do they make any discernible attempt to modify public opinion or to lobby decision makers. The voice of FE is multi-tongued and talks largely to itself. To the proverbial man or woman in the street, the variations of status which these FE agencies represent and which mean so much within the closed college sub-culture, appear meaningless. Sub-culture members may be no less varied than their prevailing-culture counterparts, but a population which knows little about the sub-culture is unlikely to display much interest in its variety.

There may be a certain cosiness in small group membership, but the effects are likely to include marginalisation, with resulting frustration and low levels of self-esteem. FE's promotional problem is that few people in the wider world outside either know much about it or care very deeply about what it does or what might happen to it. The consequent feeling of isolation is effectively summed up by one of the feasibility study respondents:

> We're so incestuous. We go to conferences to meet ourselves and to deplore the fact that nobody understands us. (Principal)

If mainstream culture usually ignores FE, FE has done little to make outsiders sit up and take notice.

Chapter 6:
College prospectuses

Even if it is largely ignored by politicians and the national media, the FE service does not rely solely on others for its image. CFEs respond to enquiries and advertise their services: both activities help to shape public attitudes.

In order to explore how FE projects itself, I collected data from several areas in which colleges are responsible for their own public images. I began with prospectuses and gathered 95 from across the country (see Appendix B for details). The Oxford English Dictionary defines prospectus as:

> A description or account of the chief features of a forthcoming work or proposed enterprise, circulated for the purpose of obtaining support.

One should therefore be able to glean from their prospectuses what colleges regard as their 'chief features', those characteristics most likely to attract potential purchasers. No less vital, what image do colleges have of their customers, since effective communication requires an understanding of the recipient as well as a plausible message?

Visual presentation

To begin with, prospectuses represent an area of promotional effort in which both general (unquantified) impression and anecdotal evidence suggest colleges have made great advances in recent years. If this is true, credit must in part be due to the marketing movement of the mid-'80s, manifested in RCP, the Marketing Network, the emergence of college marketing officers and the proliferation of marketing courses and workshops. Many colleges spend a great deal of money on prospectuses, and many staff are convinced that prospectuses are extremely important.

Anyone who has examined many educational prospectuses over the years (I first encountered them while conducting a national HE survey in the late '70s) would concede that enormous improvements have taken place in prospectus covers. The drab, poorly printed, monochrome cover is now very rare. Instead, there is considerable variety, and care has been taken to make the covers attractive. Of the 95 I collected, only 34 per cent (32) are plain (usually two colour and with the name of the college and the date); 23 per cent (22) include graphics of some sort; and 37 per cent (35) use photographs.

Innovations abound in format. Many prospectuses are now only folders, often with a pocket in the back, into which can be inserted material which relates to the recipient's interests, an arrangement which represents a move towards customisation as well as helping to reduce costs. In other instances colleges have gone for thin general prospectuses to which more specialist material can be added. There is no standard size: 47 per cent (45) of those examined are A4, 39 per cent (37) A5, and the remainder (14 per cent, 13) of diverse shapes.

The improvements, however, do not always extend beyond the cover. Visually, by far the most impressive prospectuses come – as one would hope – from art colleges. The remainder are to varying degrees problematic, and one is left wondering about the extent to which colleges have rethought these publications from inception to delivery, front to back, and to what degree they have made only superficial changes.

In many respects the current widespread use of full-colour photography is an improvement on earlier prospectuses with their murky black-and-white snapshots. However, sharply focused colour photographs are not in themselves sufficient, unless what they depict is appropriate. Subject matter remains problematic. Does one present the college as architecture or as people, or both?

Since most LEA colleges occupy unattractive (and frequently untended) buildings, some colleges resorted to cosmetic devices: windows reflecting skyscapes; the facade of buildings as viewed by a supine photographer; the building framed by spring blossom; or blurred half-tint background images. The best of this material is highly professional and often dramatic. Whether it also gives an accurate impression of the college is another matter. Whether it should is a still more interesting question.

The approach to people is far less imaginative, and it is apparent that little time has been spent on most prospectus photography which purports to show staff and students at work. Professional photographers often take several hours to light and set up a single shot. They also prefer models and actors to the real thing: most of us manage to look self-conscious and ill-at-ease when we see a camera pointed at us. Art is, after all, artificial: the real thing can look false. One wonders how many colleges have considered using professional models instead of their own frequently embarrassed students and uncomfortable middle-aged managers.

In terms of lighting, composition and subject matter most of the prospectus shots of people are amateurish and look like holiday snaps. The cropping is often inexplicable. Many students gaze directly at the camera (sometimes squinting in the sun), so that they are clearly not at work. Some photographs are dominated by equipment and furniture.

Other problems abound with the photographing of students. Too many people appear in most shots, the surroundings overshadow the people, there are too many photographs on the page, and the photographs are usually so small that they make little impact. They are also used decoratively rather than illustratively, often to break up grey text. It is very rare for a prospectus to use a photograph of a person to convey a message, i.e. to allow the image to speak more powerfully than words. One exception is the 1990/91 prospectus of Hereward College, which provides residential and daytime FE for physically disabled students. The youth on the cover and on the back, and many of the people depicted inside, come across as real personalities rather than examples.

That is exceptional. The general impression FE prospectuses convey is of students en masse, students as a crowd, in much the same way that cinema directors present the enemy in war films – from a distance and lacking in individuality. Only 13 per cent (12) of the 95 prospectuses include student comment or student profiles. Prospectus students generally have no names. They are specimens, not people.

Why should this be so? After all, scores of colleges claim to be caring, and in many instances individual teachers would doubtless be regarded as such by their students. College mission statements usually have something to say about responding to the needs of individuals. And most selling messages – about cars and houses, CDs and cinema, clothes and holidays, books and plays, food and services – aim to flatter the potential customer.

Most people want to stand out, to achieve something distinctive. Advertising messages encourage us to improve our lot. BUY: you will be better off, pay less, get more for your money, be delighted or thrilled or entertained, be admired, look and feel better, stand out, fit in – and so on. Why do college prospectuses find it so difficult to present students as individual people, Lynda and Tom, Steve and Susan?

The answer, I think, can be found by turning the cover of most prospectuses and examining the contents, wherein are laid out the 'chief features' of the 'proposed enterprise'. What we enter is the closed world of FE, the sub-culture as perceived by those who work in it, or more precisely, those who sanction the prospectus. In the sample studied, 60 per cent (57) give us either a photograph of and/or message from the principal, usually within the first page or two.

It is unlikely that anyone – least of all the principal – imagines that middle-aged managers are a big turn-on for potential students. Of principals photographed on their own, 47 per cent are smiling, the remainder not, of whom a surprising number look anything but cheerful. With upwards of 20,000 students, how many people can a manager speak to meaningfully during a year? How many graduates retain vivid impressions of their vice-chancellor or principal?

Despite any protestations to the contrary, what the prospectus is telling us is that in the sub-culture of the college the most important person is the principal, not the customer. We have entered a large, complex and elaborate bureaucracy, and the message is reinforced in various ways. Some prospectuses still give us lists of staff with qualifications – Mr M Smith, Teach Cert, Dip Geog (London), BA (OU), DSE, DSE (FE); lists of governors – A R Parr, IEng, FIELECIE, MASEE; or lists of the College Council – Prof D MacGregor, co-opted member. None of this can be construed as information which is designed to benefit the reader of the prospectus, who, according to one principal's message, can be virtually anyone:

> Whether you are a mature student thinking of expanding your horizons or developing some skills, an employer looking for a relevant short training course, or a young person about to leave school, we have something for you.

What that something might be has seldom been identified. How many ordinary people – the college's mature student, employers and young people – enter a department store or a supermarket with a burning desire for a photograph of the managing director or a list of company board members?

Finding one's way in the maze

Many colleges also seem to find it difficult to arrange their stalls in ways which might make shopping easier for the customer. The norm is still a prospectus organised in sections representing the work of departments, faculties or schools (whichever the latest college reorganisation has produced). Elaborate devices such as colour coding or coloured paper are sometimes employed to distinguish these divisions, with little apparent awareness that potential learners will be thinking in terms of subjects and courses rather than cost centres or management responsibilities. Indexes and tables of content are uncommon. Thus, an enquirer wishing to learn about catering courses might find them offered under a variety of idiosyncratic management structure heading, viz.:

- Department of Catering;
- Faculty of Business and Service Industries;
- Faculty of Creative Studies;
- Faculty of Consumer Services;
- School of Business and Professional Studies;

and computing courses might be located within:

- Department of Business and Management Studies;
- Faculty of Information Processing and Science;
- Faculty of Business Science and General Education;
- Department of Business Studies;
- Computer Centre;
- Department of Science and Mathematics;
- Faculty of Technology;

or indeed, almost anywhere in the college. Students purchase courses, not management structures. What, one might ask, is the layperson supposed to know about the distinguishing characteristics of college departments, schools, faculties and centres?

There are exceptions among the 95 examples under discussion here, but many colleges still appear to have difficulty in thinking through what they are presenting on the printed page from the customer perspective. Only 27 per cent (26) use informal names, even though it is widely known in FE that potential students are often intimidated by vast institutions, and formal names (e.g. Course Tutor– Mr GD Janney) are not welcoming. Among the 35 per cent who employ formal names, some ask the enquirer to contact a position: Applications should be made to: The Admissions Officer or Applications should be made direct to The Centre Manager, AMTEC, Unit G7, Tumble Drive, Warfarland Estate, Throckington – it would be difficult to find anything more impersonal. The remainder of the prospectus sample – 38 per cent (36) – use a mixture of informal and formal names, which suggests not only inconsistency but colleges without a clear policy (or idea) about corporate image.

There are other ways in which the majority of these prospectuses can be viewed as user-unfriendly. Most (60, or 63 per cent) offer no information about course content, class contact (82, 86 per cent), assessment (79, 83 per cent) or career prospects (61, 64 per cent). Nearly half (44, 46 per cent) tell us nothing about entry requirements. Some of these omissions may be explained by the fact that more than half (53, 56 per cent) of the prospectuses set out to provide only general information, and the enquirer may be able to learn more specific details at a subsequent enquiry or through the inclusion of added material.

One may nevertheless question what is meant by general information. More than three-quarters (74, 77 per cent) do not include a map of where the college is located or information about how to get there. With reference to fees, only 30 per cent (29) give information, 50 (53 per cent) do not and 16 (17 per cent) refer the student to another agency, usually a local authority. Colleges may not be certain of fees at the time of printing, or fees may be expected to change during the lifetime of the prospectus, but most businesses print separate price lists for insertion in their brochures.

A few of the prospectuses I examined were cheaply produced, but most suggest that the college has devoted considerable resources to the task and that professional printers have been used. Only five (five per cent) employ paid advertising to offset costs.

The kind of imaginative leap which would enable an inward-looking annual prospectus to be transformed into a customer-centred tool continues to elude many colleges. Prospectuses have become glossier and prettier, but only some have become more helpful. The result is that too many still convey messages which are beneficial to neither the college nor the customer.

Expectations and exceptions

Is one carping unduly, or expecting miracles from the ordinary FE college around the corner? I think not. The basic lessons about good prospectus construction have been much researched, written about and taught in recent years. RCP spent a substantial amount of public money to find out how colleges might make their prospectuses more effective. All of the deficiencies noted above have been fully addressed in the RCP marketing materials, and professionally designed examples of what to do and how to do it have been provided. The package has been extensively promoted and widely bought by FE colleges. Thus, at least some of the above colleges (77 per cent) which still do not provide a location map or (60 per cent) which continue to star the principal and treat students as crowd scene extras have done so by choice.

Amidst so much material that seems to have been produced by reflex action and so much communication by cliche, there does emerge from time to time an exceptional prospectus that sets standards and demonstrates possibilities. The Hereward College effort noted above provides one example. So does the Newcastle College prospectus, not included in the survey because the college did not respond to the written request by the end of the seventh week, but sent to me by a Newcastle member of staff and sufficiently interesting to merit special attention.

It has to be admitted that Newcastle's prospectus is a very expensive production, a large ring binder of unusual size (approximately 12 x 7 inches) holding one general brochure and seven subject (e.g. art and design, engineering, food and service industries) brochures, and housed in a sturdy slip case. The prospectus oozes quality. Indeed the whole is too costly for the college to make available in its entirety to individual enquirers, so its distribution has been limited to brokers (e.g. careers officers, employers), although specific brochures are offered to individuals. All of the material is general and needs to be supplemented with more detailed information about specific courses and services.

The cost (details withheld at the college's request) and the resulting limited distribution raise awkward questions. Has the college got its priorities right? Is limited distribution appropriate for a general prospectus? Would it be possible to reduce costs in subsequent editions? Because of late delivery, the prospectus was not used at the start of the academic session, so it is not yet known whether it will stimulate increased demand and thus cover its cost. At a practical level, one remains cautious, but there is still no denying that the Newcastle prospectus presents an impressive exemplar in which many of the problems noted above have been resolved.

The production was put out to tender and the best bid accepted. Printing, design work and photography have thus been done by a private-sector firm instead of being handed to a (un)willing teacher to have a first 'go', and the results show clearly how effectively professionals can tackle the job. After all, if colleges train people as printers, designers and photographers, why do they so often assume that teaching staff, managers and committees can instantly master skills for which they have neither formal training nor workplace experience?

The Newcastle prospectus is not only attractive and professional, but the usual stereotypical social, sexist and racist blunders are neatly avoided (a woman appears on the cover of the engineering brochure: point taken). Each brochure contains a map showing where the subjects under discussion are taught. Attention is drawn to the college's 'unrivalled facilities'. What we are offered is the world of the college as seen by students. Teachers are relegated to the background in photographs. Quotes from named students and employers are used as testimonials to what can be achieved in the college. We are told what happened to ex-students.

STUDYING WITH US REALLY PAYS OFF

Roy Hepburn was unemployed when he joined our BTEC National Certificate course in Social Care. Before long he got a job with Newcastle's Social Services Department. Promoted twice in his first year, he now hopes to take a professional course in social work.

Muriel Wanless, a mature student, took our RSA Teachers' course in Office Technology. Now she's one of our lecturers.

Mike Simpson and Gordon Harrison were two redundant shipping company employees when they joined one of our small business courses. Now they are (respectively) Operations Director and Operations Manager of the M/V Thorseggen, which carries newsprint from Canada to California.

Indeed, attractive as the whole production is visually, it is the writing which is most striking, in this instance clearly the work of someone with a professional background. It speaks to the customer in ordinary language and addresses matters which are of fundamental importance to students. In the general brochure, entitled **More than just a college**, we are told the following.

STUDENTS FROM ALL SORTS OF BACKGROUNDS

Though you'll see plenty of young people at college, most of our students don't come here straight from school. Half are over 20. Half are women. Most are employed. Some don't want a career...they're studying for fun. Many have set their sights on a university or polytechnic place. Some are disabled. A few rarely come into college at all, because (with our help and guidance) they're studying at home.

WE'RE FULL OF SURPRISES

At Newcastle College, we offer much more than great vocational training. We run GCSE and GCE courses in over 50 subjects, for instance. Access courses to help people get into higher education. Expert guidance for those with learning difficulties. Help with English if it's not your first language.

And you don't necessarily need formal qualifications to come here. There are many courses that require only common sense and a determination to succeed.

The text raises another interesting question. Many recent efforts to improve prospectuses have stressed the need for professional designers, printers and photographers: are professional copywriters and editors not equally vital? This does not mean that how the prospectus looks is unimportant. The document must be attractive enough to stimulate an interest in reading it, and there are still many messages which can be better conveyed through photographs and artwork than language. The Newcastle prospectus is nevertheless most impressive in the totality of its customer-centred approach, in which word and image combine to exceptional effect. It sets high standards. The next task is to explore ways of reducing the cost and of encouraging emulation.

Chapter 7:
Local newspaper college advertising and promotion

A second area in which colleges create their own image for the public is local newspapers. Indeed it could be argued that the national media considered in an earlier chapter – newspapers, periodicals and journals – represent outlets where one would not normally expect CFEs to figure prominently. FE is fundamentally a local service, traditionally run by the local authorities and intended to meet the needs of local people. Even though individual courses may recruit nationally, most provision is accessible only to those who live within the travel-to-study radius of the college, and the vast majority of students are part-time.

I therefore selected 36 local newspapers (the process and the list are set out in Appendix C) from England, Scotland and Wales. The papers were acquired for four weeks starting with Monday, 20th August 1990, which was intended to cover traditional college enrolment periods. Since this was a time when they were actively seeking students, colleges would be most likely to be advertising their services. Because of this promotional activity, the colleges might also be considered newsworthy: one might expect staff responsible for promotion and publicity to encourage local papers to run stories about the college's many opportunities and achievements.

At no point was it considered that so limited a survey could give an accurate impression of the extent to which colleges actually do advertise or are written about in their local papers. There are hundreds of papers and colleges. The one chosen from a particular town was not always the only one available, so colleges might be advertising in a rival publication. What the survey could provide, however, was a broad impression of how colleges present themselves to the public in newspaper advertisements and how local newspapers write about colleges.

College advertising in local newspapers

Of the 36 publications, only 20 contained advertisements and/or features about FE. The extent to which the papers included material about CFEs was extremely varied: at the extremes, the Somerset Express ran a single article about courses aimed at getting women into business, while the Edinburgh Herald included 20 educational advertisements and seven features.

In examining the advertisements, I included all which were for FE or any other provider who might be competing for the same potential students, i.e. polytechnics and private-sector trainers, but universities only when they were advertising for undergraduates (the same people might do a BTEC course) but not for postgraduate courses. There were 103 advertisements, 68 (66 per cent) for publicly funded institutions (including universities) and 35 (34 per cent) for private trainers, even though these, too, might be recruiting students for whom they were paid from public funds. (Government encouragement of the private sector to supply publicly funded training has blurred the tidy distinctions between public and private training: most trainers now benefit from Treasury funds.)

The above figures are somewhat misleading since they do not suggest what was clearly visible, that in excess of 90 per cent of the actual space devoted to advertisements was for FE, often in the form of whole-page advertisements, while most of the private advertisements were small one- or two-column boxes. From an income perspective, CFEs are (at least in August and September) major advertisers in these local newspapers, beside whom private trainers are relatively insignificant.

There are other differences between the two sectors. The general impression made by CFE advertisements is of large, impersonal bureaucratic institutions where the individual is likely to count for little more than a statistic. This is most noticeable in the gargantuan one- or two-page advertisements of courses (frequently run by local authorities for a number of colleges) which read and look like telephone directories. The more imaginative colleges organise these by days of the week (crucial for many potential part-time students), while the remainder approach the task either by subject areas or alphabetically, as in:

Sugarcraft (Cake Dec)	19.00-20.30	Wed
Sugarcraft	09.45-11.45	Wed
Swimming, Adult Beginner	10.30-11.15	Sun
Swimming, Par & Child (Imp)	09.00-10.20	Sun
Swimming, Beg & Impr.	17.45-18.30	Mon
Swimming, Jun Improvers	16.15-17.00	Mon
Swimming, Family Swim	09.45-10.30	Sun

which must prove overwhelming to some, especially when the above list is followed by another 41 swimming classes. Contact names are not given.

This impression of impersonality and of the subordination of the customer to the organisational requirements of the provider is strengthened by other features of FE advertisements. For example, only 16 per cent of public sector advertisers include contact names (John Smith, Mrs K. Jones) while 42 per cent of the private advertisers do so (often using only first names). One is therefore more than two-and-a-half times as likely to be given a contact name by the private agency. What one is never likely to get from the latter is the familiar public-sector requirement to seek information from an organisational structure or a room: The Registry, The Admissions Section, Student Services.

Many of the CFE advertisements are for enrolment dates and times, and these more than anything else foster the impression of being slotted into arrangements convenient to the college. Thus, while some FE colleges may actually provide whole days (10 and 11 September, 9.30 am – 8.30 pm), others are restrictive (3 September, 12–3 pm) or clearly built around staff breaks (10 am – 1 pm, 2 pm – 6 pm), as if the lunch hour were not for many potential students the best (and sometimes the only) time to enrol.

When CFEs do attempt to appear more flexible, the approach can sometimes be unintentionally comic. Thus the information that

> Depending on the course, you can study during the evening, part-time during the day or on flexible or open learning.

is only inches away from Mr Ford's famous car available in any colour, so long as it is black. Similarly with the recommendation to

> Please note that if there is sufficient demand, there will be creche facilities available on Mondays am, Tuesdays and Wednesdays am and pm, and Thursdays am.

which presumably means that if the demand for creche facilities involves Mondays or Thursdays pm or Fridays at any time, the customer had better look elsewhere or think again. Even well meaning assistance such as

> An informal drop-in service offered by experienced staff covering all courses, open to all aged 16 and over. Come early and avoid the queues!

can appear otherwise when it is followed by the information that the service is available from '10 am to 12.30 pm'. Likewise with the college which offers a 24 hour service but notes that there is only an 'answerphone after office hours', which might be useful if one could phone in an order with a plastic-card number (not possible because the college accepts only cheques).

There are exceptions. Some colleges do inform customers that 'Payments can be made with Access or Visa' (most accept only cheques or cash) and several permit postal entry to non-award-bearing courses. At other times the gesture is only half hearted: to obtain the course directory for adult leisure classes you must 'send a large stamped addressed envelope' to the college, but can do so by FREEPOST. The advertisement does not say how large is large or how much postage to include, but, then, in the business world few sales departments would ask a potential customer interested enough to respond to send an envelope for the answer. In the FE world, however, this is considerably better than being directed for the prospectus to the local library, which is how other colleges seek to distribute their prospectuses.

On the whole, the private colleges are better at conveying in their advertisements the personal, customer-centred message which FE colleges traditionally find so difficult. Private trainers are frequently well aware – in a much smaller space and at less cost – of how to communicate directly to the individual. Many mention small classes, specialist teachers and individual attention or 'Professional training with the personal touch'. One firm offers 'a free taster session on Tuesday afternoons' and training 'At times to suit YOU'. A language training company providing French and German intensive 13 week evening courses invites prospective customers to meet the teachers and 'see how we work' at two information evenings at The Pavilion Hotel, 6.00 – 8.30 pm. Such an approach has only begun to surface in the more adventurous CFEs.

Perhaps even more interesting is the way that FE colleges frequently emphasise their down-market image, as the place you go when you've failed to achieve what you really want. It is most noticeable in advertisements – some of them relatively large – for GCSE and A level re-sits. For example,

> GCSE Results Not Good Enough?
> Undecided What to Do?
> School Leavers – Parents – Need Advice?
> WE CAN HELP YOU

violates the basic tenets of advertising, that it should be positive and stress benefits. It must also discourage those (or their parents) whose GCSE results are good enough but who might like to study for A levels. In the business world, down-market suppliers emphasise low price and value for money, rather than that their customers can afford nothing better. The FE college confronting the need to attract the disappointed might try a somewhat more positive approach (used by another CFE) such as: 'Improve Your Science A levels'.

Virtually all of these advertisements (including the private-sector ones) rely exclusively on words to convey their messages, frequently supplemented by the college logo. The one exception is a two-page advertisement for community education with includes graphics, plus photographs and quotations from typical students (various ages, black and white, male and female). The tag line in all their advertisements is 'We're here to help you. Use us'.

Exceptions of this sort stand out because they are so different, not least in that they build on the practical recommendations of RCP and avoid the familiar mistakes which have bedevilled so much FE advertising in the past. By contrast, given the opportunity to control their own presentation and to influence the ways in which the public might view them, the majority of CFEs continue to present a stereotypical picture of themselves, low level, impersonal, at best an alternative to something better, expecting people to fit into what is on offer, at times and in places which suit the providers.

What seldom occurs in any of these newspapers is a CFE advertisement which is deliberately designed to enhance the college's image, rather than merely to convey information. The use of student photographs and quotations noted above is one exception. Another, even more remarkable (recently drawn to my attention and not in the survey), involves Solihull College of Technology, which on 7 December 1990 placed a full-page advertisement in its local paper (Solihull Times) informing readers that it

> ..sent 222 students to higher education this year! We thought you'd like to see details of their success. Our congratulations to every one of them, and also the 1,126 leavers who went into good jobs or further training.

The names of the students are then listed alphabetically, together with their HE destinations (institutions and courses). A banner across the bottom proclaims that: 'FURTHER EDUCATION DELIVERS THE GOODS!' 'APPLY NOW FOR COURSES BEGINNING IN 1991'.

The goal is light years away from the 'GCSE Results Not Good Enough' approach noted earlier, suggesting (but not stating directly) that Solihull College of Technology can help students get into higher education. The presentation makes the point powerfully because it is both oblique and positive, leaving the reader to draw out the inference. Of course no one will read through all of the names, but the sense of abundant student achievement is inescapable. Perhaps even more extraordinary is the reference to the 1,126 students who did not go on to HE, but are still regarded as successful, thus demonstrating that it is not necessary to denigrate one group of customers while praising another.

Local press news and features about colleges

The rather low-key, down-market impression made by so much CFE advertising is not entirely dispelled by the feature articles which local newspapers run about further education. However, the 20 papers which contain something about post-16 training and education are on the whole far more positive in their reporting of FE than FE usually is in its own presentation. Apart from the occasional gaffe which one associates with local newspapers (e.g. a marvellous new 'woodwork for old people' course), news and features about FE colleges were presented more frequently than any other kind of education/training story. Altogether there are 18 such stories about 13 colleges, two of which seem to be particularly good at getting themselves reported.

The college items cover a range of activities. Some are merely general but others concentrate on particular achievements: 31 students from a local firm who completed a language training course; a short course programme; a new local history course. Another takes the FE-isn't-what-it-used-to-be approach. The most disappointing is an advertisement feature on a college which is illustrated by a photograph of the principal and another of the entrance to the main building, obviously photographed when the college was closed, since no visible sign of student life obtrudes. Training in how to deal with the media or a college publicity officer might have prevented the college being presented as principal- (rather than student-) centred.

When students are photographed in another story, they have no names. Even when names are provided, the down-market image of FE often manages to prevail. The Edinburgh Herald and Post ran (23 August) an inside feature on two enterprising CFE students who persuaded 15 shopkeepers in William Street to pay them to promote the street by walking around with sandwich boards. The following week (30 August) the same paper offered a front page story on two university students bicycling to Moscow to raise £4,000 for charity through sponsorships. The contrasting subject matter encapsulates the way in which printed material sustains stereotypical images. CFE students also undertake sponsored activities for charity.

Compared to colleges, private-sector trainers feature far less prominently with only six articles, all of them short and at least two of them brief announcements obviously intended to coincide with nearby advertisements. The general articles (excluding schools features) cover training, the use of training videos, education for people aged 50 and above, warnings over the effect of the poll tax on education and the trials of 'red tape'.

As mentioned earlier, the volume of FE reporting varies greatly from paper to paper. The Shropshire Star, for example, ran an Education and Training supplement on 21st August, thereby providing a large number of feature articles and stimulating substantial advertising. By contrast, the Liverpool Echo, a tabloid-style paper with a large circulation, may well prefer to run stories on the poll tax, the council, football and the Beatles rather than education and training, although it did feature prominently a well known secretarial college which had received Approved Training Organisation status for employment training. Nor did CFEs feature in the Glasgow Herald and the Western Mail (printed in Wales) which are national papers covering much more than their local regions. In such papers, CFEs appear to be regarded as inconsequential and uninteresting.

Telling it like it is

Despite the exceptional advertisments noted above, the overall impression of FE which emerges from most local newspaper advertisements and features (as well as college prospectuses) is downbeat and rather dowdy, a provider-centred bureaucracy which is large but impersonal, complex and inflexible, which expects its users to fit into existing provision patterns and finds it difficult to adapt to individual requirements or expectations. The key question is whether the impression is false or accurate, the result of faulty promotional techniques and public misunderstanding, or the real truth.

Previous chapters suggest the latter. Many responses from college principals and marketing officers convey the impression that they often see themselves as being viewed unfavourably by the public and that they consider the public are frequently correct in their perceptions. The negative image, however, is also fostered and fed by the way FE projects itself. It appears to be an accurate impression of the predominant reality, which means that FE is most often genuine in the claims it advances and the service it depicts.

In the advertisements discussed above, you really cannot expect creche facilities on Mondays and Thursday pm or any time on Friday. You can study evening or part-time during the day or via open learning, but only if the course you want happens to coincide with the delivery arrangement you require. The informal drop-in service covering all courses is really available for only two-and-a-half hours in the morning, and you will almost certainly have to queue: you will not be able to make a telephone appointment to be seen at a mutually convenient time, and the college might not know how to respond if you attempted to do so. The only way you can get a prospectus is to go to the library because the college will not pay the postage. And so on.

Is this unique? Not if one is talking about providers who hold the monopoly on their services. One is likely to be treated in much the same way in public sector hospitals and libraries, or in private sector motorway service areas. Take it or leave it: there is no alternative. It is competition which forces suppliers to court customers.

Travellers will note that when they undertake a British Rail journey they are not welcomed on board personally and shown to their seats, or bade farewell when they depart. There are no staff present to answer calls for assistance, or help elderly and disabled people with their luggage. Reading matter (except in first-class carriages), film entertainment, meals and drinks are not provided as a matter of course. No one will offer you an aspirin if you have a headache. The general impression when travelling on British Rail is of herds of anonymous people being conveyed from point A to point B.

The reverse is true of airlines, which frequently offer faster, cheaper and more convenient travel than trains, but which – unlike trains – invest heavily in staff training and organise themselves to provide a customer-centred service. If you fly British Midland from London to Edinburgh, you will be offered a hot meal, wine and coffee on a journey which lasts barely an hour. That is the only way a small company can hope to compete with the airline giant who runs a shuttle service.

The differences between the customer's plane and train experiences are not due to false impressions or the failure of travel agents to convey the right messages. Instead, the differences lie in alternative values, attitudes and approaches, i.e. the differences are deliberate. Airlines have to take greater trouble with their customers because, if they do not, the customers will travel with competitors. And the quality of airline service is improving across the world, as increasing deregulation forces airlines to compete where once they were the sole providers protected by restrictive government legislation.

The FE problem is comparable, a hitherto dominant supplier entering a period of growing competition and therefore not so much in need of promoting itself differently as of learning to think and act differently. A customer-centred FE service which values its offerings and takes pride in what it sells, which is flexible and responsive in delivery, needs to emerge from within before a different image can be projected to the outside world. One cannot promote what does not exist and in so doing transform what does exist into something which is not yet there.

Chapter 8:
Small spenders in a big world

FE's promotional problem is not solely about acquiring the 'right' image. There is also a need to raise awareness among a largely indifferent or ignorant public. With growing competition, declining traditional markets and diminished central and local government support, colleges need above all else to be noticed. For a business relying on a large volume of relatively small sales, invisibility is a liability.

Moreover, marketing and promotion have a part to play not merely in bringing the CFE to public attention, but also in informing college staff of what the public wants and feels. Internal awareness raising can help in modifying work practices, products, delivery arrangements and attitudes to customers. The marketeer who can demonstrate that sales are poor because people want X instead of Y – or do not like being patronised, or cannot afford to release staff during the day – is theoretically well placed to initiate change.

On paper at least, colleges ought to be able to market and promote themselves effectively. Many offer marketing courses taught by lecturers with marketing experience. In recent years considerable public resources have been directed towards improving college marketing.

The problem which needed tackling was that colleges, if they promoted themselves at all, did so without much system or organisation. Like all commercial activities, marketing was treated by many as suspect, if not immoral. When marketing occurred, it was amateurish. A description given by a feasibility study principal of how his large college markets itself paints a vivid portrait of the traditional approach.

> The VP has a marketing interest. He has an *ad hoc* committee. The group is mostly interested in PR, advertising, publicity and printing. They're a disparate group. There's a live wire lass who teaches marketing and two adult education people. They're very entrepreneurial. They sell non-voc courses. I've grabbed people with energy and ideas. (Principal)

It was against this background of college marketing dependent on whatever unpredictable, uncontrolled and accidental enthusiasm might or might not surface that a serious attempt to professionalise college marketing arose in the 1980s.

The largest sum of government development money was spent on RCP, more than £2m intended to help colleges explore ways of marketing themselves more effectively. To increase the Programme's impact the TA funded the setting up of marketing units where they did not exist and the acquisition of desktop publishing to encourage colleges to produce more effective promotional materials. In addition, the MSC/TA put money into scores of smaller projects centred on specific aspects of college marketing or on college-employer links in particular industries. Local authorities sponsored their own projects and sometimes took over the financing of work initiated in RCP. FEU funded its own work in college marketing and FESC ran marketing courses.

In the meantime, with pump-priming money from FESC, those appointed to market the country's colleges formed the Marketing Network, an independent agency designed to encourage marketeers to share ideas, problems and solutions. As we moved into the 1990s, marketing seemed to be the movement of the moment.

The patchy growth of college marketing

RCP produced clear recommendations for college marketing units: a full-time marketing officer, a separate office, no teaching, a telephone, a secretary, a budget, and salary and status commensurate with that of at least the majority of other senior managers – as a minimum. It would be agreeable to believe that these recommendations have been universally welcomed. Unfortunately, they have not.

In the feasibility study, only half of the 50 colleges claimed to have a marketing unit, which, by definition, means that half did not. It is important to remember that the interviewing was weighted towards colleges (see Appendix A) which had expressed an interest in promoting FE nationally, so one might have expected a clear majority of respondents to reveal a positive, up-to-date approach to marketing. That they did not was surprising. Many colleges (with and without units) had adopted the traditional FE working arrangement of having a number of people devote bits of their work weeks to marketing, rather than going for a freestanding functional unit staffed by full-time professionals and comparable to a business studies or engineering department.

A common experience for those who run marketing courses is to receive complaints from college marketeers that they have the responsibility for marketing but lack the authority which would enable them to do their jobs effectively. In **Marketing the college** (Theodossin,1989a), one illustration showed the range of salary levels at which marketing officer posts in England and Wales were being advertised, from half-time Lecturer to Head of Department Grade IV. A glance through more recent job advertisements suggests that little (apart from salary scales) has changed in the past few years.

For example, in the **Guardian** weekend Jobs and Careers supplement (4 August 1990) a college with impeccable ideological credentials (an Equal Opportunities employer uninterested in age, disability, marital status, race or gender, and committed to a No Smoking Policy) offers a salary negotiable to £17,000 for a marketing manager who will

> ....be able to demonstrate the personal qualities required for effective communication and have experience and qualifications in marketing, materials production and public relations. Previous applicants will automatically be considered.

The last line summarises the predicament neatly at a time when salary scales reach to £18,285 for lecturers and to £22,068 for senior lecturers. One needs to remember that the effective marketing of a multi-million-pound enterprise, which most colleges have become, cannot be encompassed (as can teaching, apparently) in 38 weeks per annum and no more than 30 hours per week.

Evidence from the Marketing Network suggests that college marketing posts have become stepping stones for staff on their way to better paid employment. Why should anyone want to remain in a job whose status is not commensurate with its needs and whose pay does not reflect its responsibilities? The faster the rate of turnover in college marketing posts and the slower colleges are in developing a marketing career structure, the longer it will take for college marketing to work effectively.

The feasibility study revealed little that was more encouraging with regard to marketing budgets. Of the 50 colleges and two local authorities involved, 31 (60 per cent) said they had a marketing budget and 21 (40 per cent) did not. What those who responded positively thought of as a marketing budget was extremely variable.

Some principals appeared to operate invisible budgets. At an interview where three respondents were present, in reply to a question about whether the college had a marketing budget, the principal unlocked a cupboard and produced a notebook in which he looked up the budget. The other two respondents, both involved in college marketing, thus for the first time learned what the budget was. In a second college, a respondent observed,

> We do have one, but we don't know what it is. We spend until we're told we've spent enough, but we're not hard up. (College marketing officer)

Another suggested something similar.

> I spend until I'm told to stop. I spend as much as I can quickly. (College marketing officer)

It is difficult to imagine a successful business run in a comparable manner, or an FE business studies course that advised a budding business person to follow so strange a practice. Part of the explanation may be a deep-rooted sense of shame at spending money on anything so improper as marketing. What would people say and think if they knew? At least that seems a likely explanation for three interesting observations.

> We do have one [a budget], but we're refusing to acknowledge it. It's £8,000 and it's not enough. (Assistant principal, marketing)

> We have a budget of £3,000 to £4,000, about 10 per cent of our total income from self-financing work. But we really spend about £20,000 on marketing. Much of this is actually hidden under other budget headings. (Principal)

> We don't have a marketing budget, but I've been trying to get one for two years. We will have one in 1990-91. (Principal)

If not shame, at least anxiety seems to underlie such approaches. In theory, if local authorities are running their schools and colleges satisfactorily, there will be no competition for students, since supply and demand will be balanced. In reality, college, school and LA politics (as well as free trade across boundaries) have often resulted in intense unofficial competition among public sector providers. There is consequently understandable college concern that making public the amount of money spent on marketing could cause an outcry: immediate protests from competitors that public money was being 'wasted', and in the longer run a reduction in LEA resourcing.

Colleges are wary. One which introduced a glossy colour brochure encouraging school leavers to study for A levels at college aroused local headteachers to complain of 'unfair' competition. Another, whose prospectus was noted in an earlier chapter, was willing to reveal 'off the record' how much it had spent, but did not want the figure published. If those who are prepared to devote substantial resources to college marketing see open commitment as potentially dangerous, marketing itself remains suspect, as indeed it still is among many educationists. So long as colleges retain their present relationships with LEAs, part way between dependency and autonomy, marketing can flourish only through exceptional confidence and commitment. And when it does, flak will almost certainly fly.

In some colleges, marketing is still thought of solely in terms of selling, and what actually passes for a marketing budget is in fact an advertising budget, i.e. the amount being spent on the prospectus, leaflets and occasional inserts in the local paper.

> We have a publicity budget. (College marketing officer)

> We have an advertising budget, and I'm prepared to find supplementary funding. (Principal)

This willingness to dip into other budgets to increase meagre allocations seems commonplace and is another manifestation of the instinct to bury actual costs by dispersing them among cost centres. Six of the Scottish colleges which were visited exhibited varied, but hardly substantial, advertising budgets: £2,800; £3,000; £4,500; £8,000; £13,600 and £15,000. Most appeared prepared to supplement these amounts, if necessary.

Two English principals nonetheless revealed that they had relatively (for colleges) large marketing budgets.

> We will spend about £30,000 for 1990-91. (Principal)

> Last year I spent £50,000 on marketing. It certainly had an effect, but it was nowhere near enough to raise awareness. (Principal)

Both appeared to be exceptional. By far the majority of colleges find the whole business of a marketing budget somewhat uncomfortable. Among college managers, marketing is still not universally regarded as altogether respectable – or even absolutely necessary.

The by-ways of off-beat college promotion

Previous chapters examined the more traditional ways of promoting the college (prospectuses, advertisements), but colleges have also begun to explore some unconventional approaches. When it comes to off-beat promotion, colleges can be remarkably enterprising, but generally they confine their activities to the cheaper end of the market. Thus they usually go for paper and paper-related products (logos on sticky note pads, folders, pencils, calendars, business cards, rubbers, bookmarks, diaries, paper clips, Christmas cards, etc.). Beer mugs and beer mats remain controversial (they can be seen as lively or vulgar), as do shopping bags (£250 for 10,000 can be a convenient way of producing hundreds of walking advertisements). Such artefacts tend to inspire strong emotions. As one respondent put it,

> I loathe that sort of thing. But if everyone else is doing it, I suppose we'll have to. (Principal)

It is noteworthy that between a fifth and a quarter of interviewees rejected shopping bags, rulers and T-shirts, but a smaller proportion (15 per cent) opposed key fobs, presumably because they are usually invisible (which defeats the purpose of the promotional activity).

The above responses formed the part of the feasibility study in which the 62 respondents were asked to answer Yes, Maybe or No as to whether they might be interested in purchasing a range of promotional materials. The most popular item (65 per cent Yes; 10 per cent No) was radio advertisements which many colleges already use. These give the college opportunities to link in with local stations, particularly in the traditional autumn recruiting period – and to use professional broadcasters for a relatively modest cash outlay.

One college had spent £1,300 on Capital Radio advertising, which should have enabled it to reach 15 per cent to 18 per cent of the 16-24 age group (approximately a quarter of a million local people) in nine or 10 spots. Another spent £1,200 for 30 spots per week for a fortnight using a 30-second tape during periods just before examinations and overlapping the exam results announcements. Although respondents showed considerable interest in purchasing TV advertisements (58 per cent Yes; only 18 per cent No), these are enormously costly, and currently outside the reach of virtually every college.

College videos were generally popular among respondents, with significant proportions interested in purchasing (in order of decreasing enthusiasm, from 71 per cent to 50 per cent Yes) videos aimed at school leavers, women returners, employers, adults in need of retraining and updating and access course students. School leavers might have been expected to be most popular since many colleges have begun using them in recent years. Another potential area for development is the overseas video: 63 per cent of respondents expressed an interest in overseas marketing, and a video is the obvious and portable way of taking an impression of the country, the region, the local area and the college to other lands.

In the past, one of the main college video difficulties has been amateurism. Most videos are produced entirely by the college, and the worst exhibit the conventional features associated with prospectuses: the principal in the leading role (often a bobbing head reading unconvincingly from a stilted script without the advantage of idiot cards), content organised by management divisions, stiffness and formality etc. Sometimes other liabilities are introduced, such as total reliance on stills photography to reduce costs or a throbbing pop background, suitable for some audiences but alienating to others.

The most impressive college video I have seen to date was produced by an Australian college. The filming and editing were done by the college video unit, but a professional scriptwriter (the key element in any conceptualisation) was used and local TV presenters were employed to front the video. Staff are present only in the background and the emphasis throughout is on students.

British colleges frequently do all promotional work in-house instead of collaborating with professionals and ensuring that inside knowledge and outside presentational skills join to create the best possible effect. The conventional reason has been money. Given their traditional funding formulae, CFEs have found it easiest to give teaching staff remission from the classroom rather than to spend (sometimes less) money on buying assistance. At the time of the feasibility study, many respondents had not yet grasped the potentialities of devolved financial control which include the option of viring money across budget headings, thus enabling private sector providers to be bought in for specialised tasks such as video production.

Another difficulty which colleges have encountered with videos is a paucity of ideas about how to use them. Generally there are two approaches: taking the video to a school whose pupils do not visit the college; and showing the video at an open day, when it has to compete (often unsuccessfully) with the crowds and the movement. Using a video within a darkened theatre (now increasingly common with art exhibitions) as a delayed entrance allowing visitors to be given an overview and orientation is something I have not yet encountered in a college. Nor do I know of a college which regularly uses a small portable video on employer visits or which has made a video aimed at employer groups who are not visiting the college. One can also negotiate the placement of videos for borrowing in local libraries, video shops and travel agents (they lend their own), and for viewing in trade exhibitions, where employers are looking for the latest bright ideas to help their businesses function more profitably.

Compared to businesses with a similar annual cash turnover, most colleges remain small spenders, anxious that no one should find out how much public money is devoted to marketing. Caution, however, has not necessarily precluded all adventurousness, particularly if the required cash outlay is not too large. Some of the feasibility study colleges exhibited considerable flair in searching for novel promotional venues.

One college for example, had spent £765 on a one-minute video for showing 400 times in shopping centres in November and January and £920 for a five-minute video on the college for open evenings and for overseas work, neither the mark of a big spender but both more enterprising than is as yet usual. Another paid £2,000 for 3,000 posters (four different ones) and used a professional photographer. A third college had just spent £8,000 on display boards and a fourth had signed a contract with a UK student head-hunting firm which would be paid on a fee-per-enrolment basis.

Individual respondents wanted help with setting up student services, locating freelance local journalists, and obtaining up-to-date information about the current state of marketing research – all of which suggested a willingness to pay for consultancy services. One college claimed to be willing to spend up to £10,000 on a marketing audit 'dependent on depth and content'.

Taking risks in the new marketing world

Even where external difficulties are not present, the financial implications of marketing cause college anxiety. Providing the marketing unit with the resources and authority required to make it effective – giving it the status and power it would wield in a comparable private sector firm – is still a daring move that many college managers find uncomfortable. Caution, amateurism and ad-hocery prevail more often than they should, even when the enthusiasts who are willing and able to deliver a more effective service are waiting in the wings.

Technically, as has been noted, many of the monetary constraints belong to the past. The financial delegation which has followed the Education Reform Act enables colleges to control their money (including viring) in ways that would have seemed impossible in the past. For decades, colleges and local authorities have been able to blame one another for obstructions, passing the buck backwards and forwards. The excuse is disappearing.

If, as planned, incorporation arrives in colleges in April 1993, there will be even less to constrain the development of more professional approaches to marketing and the use of more specialist staff, both as full-time appointments and in as part-time assistance bought in from the private sector. Incorporation itself will necessitate the establishment of non-teaching support staff to replicate many services currently provided by LEAs. One may anticipate that company secretaries, site managers and personnel officers will become fairly commonplace in CFEs. Colleges will also need to employ accountants and solicitors whose skills they are most likely to purchase on a part-time basis. With an increase in management task differentiation, the professionalism of marketing may seem less radical.

In the meantime, colleges can determine their own staffing levels. They can reduce the number of teachers and increase the number of support staff. They can also use teachers solely for teaching and buy in less expensive assistance. They can accumulate cash and carry over money from one financial year to the next. They therefore have the freedom to establish marketing units, and to staff and resource them properly. They can also promote themselves as they wish. Behind the Education Reform Act has been the Government's determination to force colleges into the market-place and to make them compete for survival. The problem is thus no longer technical or legal. What often appears to be lacking for its resolution is senior management conviction and the confidence to face changes and take risks.

Chapter 9:
What image does FE want to project?

The image is the shibboleth of success in the 20th century. In order to sell goods, services or ourselves, we need the 'right' image.

Whole industries exist solely to help us. They assume that most people pass judgement on the basis of limited information. We may spend six months on a house purchase and may even pay a surveyor to tell us the worst, but virtually everything else is a form of impulse buying, even if some impulses surface more slowly than others. Because in-depth research precedes few sales, first impressions are vital. Controlling initial information, so that what others see reassures them, is therefore the most effective way of achieving our goals.

Packaging as the message

British politics has been transformed in the past decade through image manipulation. We have had a (now resigned) prime minister who has been taught not to wear hats so as to shed her middle-aged, middle-class image and to drop the pitch of her voice in order to sound less shrill. The opposition leader has taken to wearing dark suits (presumably to appear middle-aged and middle-class) and his party has adopted a red rose as its emblem, ostensibly to appear less militant. Within the first week of taking office, a new prime minister has been judged to have a serious image problem: investigative journalists have identified hair, suits and glasses as requiring immediate attention.

The televising of Parliament has produced work for image consultants who teach MPs how to dress and how to powder their balding pates so as to convey a 'cooler' image to home viewers. Ministers talk about the importance of 'presentation' in putting across policies, and for a very good reason: floating voters, not the party faithful determine election results, and floating voters are, by definition, impulse buyers. Packaging has replaced the medium in conveying the message.

The image, as with Mrs Thatcher's vocal transformation, is not always visual. Sound, smell, touch and taste may play a part, even if less often. If the 'look' of the thing usually seems most crucial, it is probably because ours is a visual age, and for most of us sight is the best developed of our senses. Strawberry growers argue that what berries look like matters more to buyers than how they taste. Modern roses (pace the Labour Party) may be attractive but are seldom scented. Smile, smile, smile is the universal exhortation. Even telephonists are encouraged to beam when conversing with unseen callers, who should be able to 'hear' the difference. Sales staff are taught to touch the client's hand as they relinquish receipts or parcels: tactical contact stimulates the sensation of warmth and caring.

Overall, we are becoming increasingly conscious of how we are judged and of how the wrong impression can affect us adversely. We have the power to influence how others see us. Only fools ignore their images. Wise men and women package themselves carefully.

Cynics and intellectuals are quick to point out – quite rightly – that an initial impression may be false. If not everything we read is true, neither is everything we see.

The first impression is, nevertheless, important because the recipient lacks any other information about us. What s/he sees and experiences is a statement addressed to her/him, however unwittingly: it is silent and seldom commented upon, a way of communicating without words, but probably more powerful because it is unvoiced. It satisfies or contradicts expectations. Making a 'good impression' is therefore about allaying uncertainties, answering unasked questions, and communicating what one's audience wants to learn. If we make a bad impression, we may be able to overcome it, but not without costly time and effort.

The cultivation of images

All of the above assumes that contact has been made and that an image has been cultivated: someone has set out to make an impression and someone else has received it. The recipient has evidence in the form of direct experience.

In some instances the original creator of the cultivated image has long since moved on, but the message continues to be sent. In the public sector, vestiges of yesterday's cultivated images litter the landscape, often conveying now inappropriate messages based on assumptions which were once considered valid. We can receive such messages in antiquated hospitals, schools, town halls, libraries and train carriages. Outdated stock figures prominently in the imagery of British public life. It tells us a great deal about yesterday's values and attitudes.

One suspects that, in contrast to the image-conscious commercial world, few colleges have had access to (or have necessarily sought) the resources needed for modifying their inherited images and promoting new ones. In many instances, virtually everything which goes to make up the college image – physical plant, furnishings and fittings, working practices, attitudes, approaches, assumptions – dates from an earlier age.

Difficult as it may now be to believe, someone must have decided that the flimsy buildings, the scarcity of signposts, the dim lighting, the matchstick furniture, the barricaded and usually well hidden receptionist and the uncarpeted floors were actually appropriate for a college. Many colleges have learned to live with what they have received. Few have made concerted efforts to identify (never mind research) the kind of image which might now be appropriate.

Students, on the other hand, have frequently worked at cultivating college images. The litter and squalor which are so frequently encountered in public areas of CFEs are both a reaction and an assertion. Open messages about the college are being delivered. By contrast, staff time devoted to cultivating college images has often gone into transforming more private areas: the principal's study, the governing body meeting room and the training restaurant (where the 'right' image is arguably part of the training).

There are exceptions, such as traditional open days or one-off visits by distinguished personages, when college staff strive collectively to put on an impressive and welcoming show. More recently, colleges have sought to cultivate images through the use of logos and a range of promotional artefacts such as prospectuses, leaflets and local newspaper advertisements, but little of this has been researched in advance, and few colleges bring in professionals to assist them or – more to the point – undertake a systematic analysis of customer response so as to gauge the impact of their efforts. It is also only in the past few years that some colleges have turned their attention to the larger field of customer contacts and begun to seek advice on how better to answer the telephone, receive callers or produce promotional literature – how to create an image which shows the college in a favourable light.

The many faces of market segmentation

There are good reasons for the reticence which colleges have displayed towards deliberate image projection. When it comes to cultivating an image of itself, the college confronts a complex problem: except possibly for monotechnics, there is not one single image which could be described as appropriate for the whole college. Most colleges serve a bewildering variety of markets.

The same individual can project totally different images at, for example, the Friday morning committee meeting and the Saturday evening party, or doing jobs around the house and attending the annual company dinner. The settings and the audiences are different. One does not expect to meet the committee while decorating the family bathroom. College activities are not so conveniently separated.

The college has equally diverse audiences – school leavers and business people, pensioners and young parents, unwaged and employed adults – but it generally operates within the same setting. If it creates a casual and informal atmosphere to attract 17 year olds, it may be putting off the local manager who wants training for mid-career, senior staff. On the other hand, the kind of four-star hotel setting which may delight managers from local firms may well intimidate school leavers. The college dilemma is that it needs simultaneously to present different images to different markets.

In the business world, anyone faced with the need for such differentiation might expect different accommodation, sales staff, promotional material and budgets. Many industries market distinctive and different examples of the same good or service – cars, cosmetics, holidays – targeted at different audiences. Department stores often organise themselves in boutiques: cheap-and-cheerful clothing on the ground floor, couturier clothing on an upper floor; self-assembly furniture in one section, reproduction traditional furniture elsewhere. The underlying principle is separateness.

The essence of such division is that it assumes that each product range will be promoted as required for the appropriate market. No holiday firm, for example, would think in terms of a brochure covering opera in Vienna and Salzburg, the beach at Rimini, camping in Provence, art treasures of China, and time-shares in Minorca. The same people would be unlikely to be interested in everything, and expensive holidays would make the less costly ones look second-rate. One might also be able to devote more resources to promoting more costly holidays. Apart from being both confusing and offputting, giving all the information to everyone would put up overall costs. Holiday firms, therefore, segment the market. CFEs often find it difficult to do so.

Colleges, particularly the split-site variety, could in theory function in distinct and separate areas, each differently resourced and seeking to create a unique ambiance.

Sometimes there actually are striking differences between sites, but these are seldom deliberately contrived in order to meet varied customer needs. Generally the best cared for site is the one where most senior managers are located.

Moreover, many college staff find it difficult to accommodate the idea that one part of the college should be carpeted and furnished with lounge chairs and curtains, while another part provides little more than the low-cost plastic minimum. Where college companies have hived off one part of the college and transformed it to meet the business community's expectations, the ensuing resentment of those left in less salubrious surroundings has provided problems for management. The reason is that many staff are committed to an egalitarian political ethic: a practice which promotes economic disparity is unacceptable. In any event, business and the business ethic are not always welcome in some parts of the average college staffroom.

If it is to transform an unflattering image into a more helpful one, the college needs to know what is is aiming at. Image cultivation requires conceptualising where one is and where one would like to be. Successful image transformations – consider the modifications of Thatcher and Kinnock – derive from a clear idea of what the new image is designed to achieve. The best way of identifying the end is to try to identify in a few words – and one, if possible – just what impression one wishes to make: academic? Casual? Technically advanced? Friendly? Vocational? Adult? Youth orientated? Businesslike? And so on... Each one excludes some of the others. No one college can hope to be all convincingly at the same time and in the same place.

Moreover, if the image modification, once identified, is to be effective, it will almost certainly be necessary to seek some way of presenting the image visually. That means thinking consciously (or paying someone else to do so) about colour, a house style, the physical plant, staff attitudes, staff dress, customer contacts – all of which reinforce the image. It also means putting resources into the transformation, and colleges have usually been less well endowed financially than national political parties.

Someone should tell them

In the feasibility study, it was important not merely to find out how respondents thought the college was perceived, but also if they themselves wished to see those perceptions altered. They were consequently asked, How would you like to see FE's image changed, if at all? Respondents usually answered the question at some length. Some had clear-cut views of a positive or negative nature. Others were ambivalent and chose to explore what they saw as a complex and difficult problem, at one moment aware of positive developments and at another conscious of persistent dilemmas.

A large group of respondents suggested that FE's negative image often derived from public ignorance, that potential customers were unaware of the changes that had occurred and of the high quality of much college provision. The colleges had been transformed, but customer attitudes had not.

> Among employers and parents the image is of what they knew 25 years ago. (LEA marketing officer)

Many respondents felt that FE was poor at communicating news of its achievements to others.

> It needs a much higher profile. We need to tell people of our successes. (Assistant principal, marketing)

> There's a need to ensure that our comprehensive and responsive nature is put over more fully. You can do combinations of subjects. Access should be promoted. We don't make enough of what we do. (Assistant principal)

> I'd like to see it getting more publicity and more TV air time. I'd like to see more success stories. It's far too low profile, too down market. (College publicity officer)

Two respondents were very specific about the kinds of false impressions of FE which survived.

> FE needs more emphasis on being open 50 weeks a year. We had 1,200 workers from a local works this summer for the first time. There's still a feeling that at the beginning of July everybody disappears for eight weeks. (Principal)

> I'd like to see the image changed in the direction of greater efficiency. We are fairly efficient, but that's not the image. (Principal)

In particular, there was a belief that employers perceived the colleges inaccurately, that their image of CFEs was outdated and invalid.

> Employers don't know what technologies are being offered. Of course employers haven't kept up-to-date with qualifications, but it's the colleges who are responsible. (Principal)

The ideal would be to convey the reality, that we're able to offer a wide range of employer services. We need a higher awareness in the community. (Principal)

We ought to be aiming at a situation where an employer who has an education and training need will think of us first. The older ones think of FE as night school. (Principal)

We ought to be viewed in terms of one-stop training access. (Principal)

A small number of observations involved the failure of customers to recognise how much advanced academic work could be found in CFEs. Only two respondents touched on this issue.

It can also do pretty high level management training, information technology. You can get to university through FE. (College marketing officer)

It should be promoted so that people were aware of the range of things that could be done. The vocational courses and BTEC are publicised, but FE can also lead to university or polytechnic entrance. FE should be glamourised a little bit more. It needs more respectability in the academic field, not the idea that if people aren't doing well in school they can go to FE. (College marketing officer)

In a promotional agency, the kinds of required image modification identified above would be regarded as routine work. Changing customer perceptions is usually possible, given enough determination and money. Much more difficult to confront are the modified social, cultural and political standing which some respondents desired.

I'd like it to be seen as a very important sector of the economy and education provision. I'd like to see it valued and understood, promoting the reskilling of Britain. It needs to be given prominence. I think we're doing it well. I'd like to see the complex nature of our business a bit more understood. (Principal)

I'd like to see our worth and value come over more clearly. (College marketing officer)

There's a multi-million pound enterprise called FE which can deliver well. I'd like recognition that that's the natural resource of VET. I'm not sure it's recognised. I'd like to see greater national focus, a network of colleges. (Principal)

Paying for the job

For another group of respondents, FE's image problem is closely related to resources. To some, the difficulty centred on being required to make do with inadequate funding. If FE is going to improve its image, it needs money. FE has a dowdy image because it is dowdy, and it is dowdy because it lacks money.

> The college used to be clean and well kept. We've been privatised and we now have 50 per cent fewer cleaning staff. (College marketing officer)

The embarrassment of unattractive decor was noted by another respondent.

> We should provide a comprehensive and welcoming service for everyone, and be bright and modern and glitzy with it! I hesitate to bring visitors into the college: how can I get to my office without going through the college? (Principal)

One might have anticipated more such complaints, but other respondents were unexpectedly reflective about the funding issue. One, for example, wondered whether education in general suffered from too much government funding.

> There's ignorance of the value of BTECs. It's tied up with the way we treat education. Although I hate to admit it, maybe it's because education has been free or relatively cheap that it's not valued. (Associate principal, marketing)

Another believed that FE's poor image resulted from its failure to keep pace in a rapidly changing technological world.

> There's a resources problem... Think of new technology in commercial organisations – automated offices and CAD CAM – and you can see that colleges are not keeping pace. FE needs some investment. (Principal)

There was also an awareness that customers needed to perceive what they were buying as providing value for money

> FE needs to increase responsiveness, to establish a reputation for value-added and quality in what it does. (Principal)

I'd like FE to be seen as giving value for money, excellence and quality. We make noises but we have a long way to go. (Vice-principal, marketing)

and that in order to achieve the required changes, the college would have to charge customers substantially more.

I'd like to see us promoted as attempting to match provision to clients, offering customised training. High profits are needed. (Principal)

Changing content as well as packaging

The latter respondents could also be seen as fitting into another group who believed that FE's image problem derived not from public ignorance but from FE's failure to make requisite changes. FE needed to transform itself before it could alter its image. These respondents emphasised that many of the FE criticisms which emerged during the 1980s were still valid. Rigidity and slowness were noted as features which ought to be transformed.

I'd like it to be adaptable and quick to respond. (College marketing officer)

As flexible, adaptive, dynamic, buzzy, but also trying to be welcoming and supporting. (Principal)

Another respondent believed that FE did not compare favourably with the private sector.

I'd like to see FE able to compete with commercial organisations. I've just come from business, and I think FE doesn't compete. (College marketing officer)

At the heart of the FE problem was a perceived lack of professionalism among staff and the absence of a management information system capable of identifying problems.

It needs an effective quality assurance system so people can pick up where it's going wrong and do something about it...It needs better presentation of its image: less restrictive working practices, flexible delivery, improved administration, more admin staff, more money spent on presentation. (Assistant principal, marketing)

> I'd like to see professionalism in the way we deliver and competence of individual lecturers within specialisms. (Principal)

> There are always complaints about the phone. We need a more 'professional' image, a welcoming approach to the college. We ought to be ensuring that lecturing staff are there for lecturing and not expensively carrying out routine clerical jobs. We ought to be increasing support staff. We need to be seen as professional, receiving and welcoming. (Principal)

How far should colleges go towards professionalism? According to one respondent quite far, but not to the extent of embracing the business ethic totally.

> We should do away with 'FE'. It should be dropped from brochures. We should be more businesslike and we should be run as a business, but not for profit. (Vice-principal)

From a lone voice there was an interesting prediction, that in the long run the appropriate image would be created and sustained by neither external agencies nor colleges themselves. Instead, the market would decide.

> Over a period of 10 years you'll see successful colleges take off. I suspect we'll be down to between 200 to 250 successful ones. That will improve the image. (Principal)

Can FE provide for everyone?

The principle of department store differentiation has been noted earlier, but it also needs to be observed that many well known chains practice market segmentation not only internally, but also by not attempting to cater for everyone in any one store. Multi-nationals like Marks and Spencer and Sainsburys run stores with different levels and grades of provision, based on the socio-economic characteristics of the local population. This means that unless the community is totally homogeneous some sections will find themselves not well catered for because the provider cannot meet everyone's needs.

There is also the problem that with the proliferation of goods derived from the many overseas manufacturers who now market their wares in Britain, there is a corresponding decrease in the number of providers who can be genuinely comprehensive in what they stock. The small specialist shop has become a growth area, and in recent years many retailing outlets (e.g. in clothing, music, furniture) have turned towards specialisation, while department stores rent floor space to individual suppliers, so that the result resembles an oriental bazaar more than a conventional Western store.

The creation of college companies has represented a movement in precisely this direction, with specific provision syphoned off for individual treatment, and consequently a recognition that different markets need to be catered for differently. Some college managers have seen the company as being superceded by the Education Reform Act, because the latter gives colleges delegated financial control, but in so doing they have assumed that such companies have been started solely to facilitate greater financial flexibility for the college. In fact, they also make it easier for a part of the college to market itself separately and in so doing to circumvent some of the ensuing problems which derive from ideological objections noted above.

Private-sector trainers may have broadened their range of offerings (Theodossin, 1989a) but they have not attempted to encompass anything as diverse as FE. In its most extreme form, the same college offers everything from YTS to first degree work, and there are signs that this variety is likely to increase in at least some CFEs. The current emphasis on raising HE participation is encouraging polytechnics to franchise degree work to FE colleges, with the result that the portfolio of FE offerings is expanding.

Despite the trend towards diversity, there remains the problem about the extent to which FE can sustain so broad a range of training and education for what are effectively quite distinct and separate market segments. One group of respondents was clearly committed to diversity and did not appear to have any qualms about the kinds of promotional and delivery problems which this entailed.

> I'd like it to be seen as a much more flexible resource for the community, all segments: employers, the elderly, the unemployed, school leavers, schools themselves...a place where individuals are looked after and cared for. (Principal)

> I'd like employers to see us as... prepared to talk to them and meet their needs. I'd like local people – the unemployed and those who need education enhancement – to think of colleges and a community resource. (Principal)

> I'd like to see more involvement with industry. I'd like us to be seen as a source for updating. We need more active project work...I wouldn't like FE to lose its links with the community. We're part of the community, but we have more than one function. (Principal)

While maintaining the same commitment to many markets, one respondent acknowledged some current concerns,

> FE should be promoted as a whole, as they do with farming, but you also need to raise the profile of sections without a good reputation. (College marketing officer)

One principal saw diversity as both desirable and attainable.

> I'd like to see different images for different customers. We ought to be seen as a mature environment for adults doing updating, and as caring for school leavers (guidance staff, tutors). I want to see the view that I have the best equipment here. They have the toys, but we have the real McCoy. (Principal)

Two other respondents affirmed their commitment to wide-ranging FE offerings but implied their preparedness to limit employer provision in the direction of specialisms.

> I'd like it to be more of a community centre as well as highly specialised for particular industries. (Principal)

> It needs to differ for different sectors. Employers ought to be working with us in partnerships. We should be offering high tech, off-campus training and do consultant specialising, not the broad-brush, we-can-do-anything approach. With adults we ought to provide a community environment, almost a social facility, with life enhancement opportunities and re-direction changes in your life – for women returners, the handicapped, and so on. With the 16+ market we should be seen as offering areas where you can progress vocationally because we offer specific, tailor-made training. (LEA marketing officer)

Other respondents believed that FE could not effectively deliver all of the offerings it is traditionally supposed to provide: specialisation was inevitable.

> I'd like to see a clearly designated range of target groups...There should be more clarification about what the individual college should see as its role. (Principal)

> We've got to get to individuals to convince them that we can deliver in a limited number of areas, and deliver work that is relevant. (Principal)

> We need a sharper focus on the specific services FE offers. It doesn't have a clear image. There's no unique selling proposition. There are too many selling propositions, and they get in each other's way. (Principal)

One respondent implied that both breadth and specialisation could possibly be accommodated by effective presentation. Image was perhaps something of the magician's art.

> If you widen the appeal too much, you may not satisfy anyone. The trick is to look like a specialist. (Principal)

Which is, of course, what market segmentation is all about: convincing every potential customer that the CFE can satisfactorily meet his or her individual and unique needs.

Chapter 10:
Improving FE's image

FE's position in the educational market-place is generally accepted as problematic. There is widespread agreement about desired ends: a higher profile, increased recognition, improved quality, growth and development. What is lacking is effective solutions. Feasibility study respondents were therefore asked, What, if anything, do you think could or should be done to improve FE's image?

Taking a national perspective

At this point we ought to recall the context in which the question was put. Before being asked anything, respondents were told about the projected work of the (then) proposed FE Marketing Unit: it was intended to promote FE nationally and to co-ordinate local promotional work with national campaigns.

In the circumstances, many respondents might have been expected to see FE as needing national promotion, particularly of the kind which the Unit might provide. Only five did so. While all of their responses affirmed that a central voice was important for FE, they revealed different ideas about how it might speak. One respondent wanted an agency which would represent colleges when 'a voice' was required.

> We need an organisation to give a form to us nationally. It would be useful to have a general awareness from industry that a voice spoke for FE. Employers have the CBI and other employer networks, chambers of commerce... a national voice is the next move we should be aiming at. (Principal)

A second person stressed the need for awareness raising.

> FE needs national advertising and information, not just promotional activities. It ought to inform people of what it has to offer to various age groups, from trainees to professionals. (College marketing officer)

Two others suggested that TV and cinema advertising were appropriate, while a fifth acknowledged the usefulness of a national voice, but was also concerned to make changes within colleges.

> At national level we need a voice. We should stand up and be counted. There's also a lot of work that needs doing with internal problems. We don't always offer a quality service. We need to put our house in order. (Associate principal, marketing)

Action at college level

Do colleges really need to put their house in order? Not everyone agreed. One respondent, for example, suggested that he had already cracked the problem.

> The answer is in what we're doing. We've appointed staff with responsibility for community liaison and for industrial liaison. We've spent money on more advertising and awareness raising. Our prospectus is user friendly and accessible. We've changed the letterhead. I hate to use advertising jargon, but our corporate image is one of welcoming. We go into schools. We run link courses. We do joint schemes with school teachers. We house the careers service. We have slick, well thought through, but casual publicity materials. (Principal)

Four other respondents identified customer ignorance rather than supplier deficiency as the problem. They reiterated familiar arguments about out-of-date employer perceptions and a failure to appreciate how hard college staff work.

> We need to show people through advertising. We need success stories that can be promoted: if you go to FE and work hard you can be a leader, a company manager. (College marketing officer)

All publicity, even bad publicity, has its uses.

> Baker's Cinderella speech was helpful even if it reinforced the image I'm against, but FE was at least mentioned. FE is often forgotten. (Principal)

Another respondent claimed to be doing everything that marketing and promotion experts had advised.

> We've made a massive attempt to get more people in. We've run open evenings for district councillors. We ran an open evening on

1992 and invited 127 employers; 47 came. We've put the borough crest on our stationary and had a launch to celebrate the event. I'm now a member of the mayor's industry committee. (Principal)

Such claims, however, were exceptional. Most respondents believed that FE's problems were to be found at college level, which was where action was required. A large group was convinced that the only way to improve FE's public image was to change the staff. The most extreme respondent suggested, in response to the question about what could be done, that it was primarily her peers who were at fault.

> You could start by sacking half the principals and getting people in their place with some gumption... Everyone's been to schools and understands what they do. Most people working in FE haven't been to FE. My CEO hasn't yet visited my college! (Principal)

Not only principals and chief education officers, but much less elevated managers could also be unsatisfactory.

> Management below senior level is crucial. LEAs think we're only here to teach. If we're going to be efficient, we need to concentrate on management below the senior level. (Vice-principal, marketing)

A number of respondents welcomed the opportunity to tell an outsider about the limitations of their subordinates. One saw widespread inefficiency and idleness.

> Our staff are out of date. They're lethargic. Some of them after 50 are not too keen to change...12 weeks' holiday is a piece of damned nonsense...We'll have to get our act together or sack 90 per cent of the actors and get new ones in. That's not to say that they're not capable, intelligent, and adaptable people, but 40 per cent to 50 per cent of the FE workforce think FE exists so they can pay mortgages and have holidays abroad. (Principal)

Another principal wanted more control over staff deployment.

> Local FE principals need to be given greater flexibility over staff conditions of service. (Principal)

For an assistant principal the snag was a rigid and bureaucratic system which espouses enterprise culture goals but finds if difficult to reward achievement.

> I took over an ET agency here and made £157,000 in seven months. We upped the publicity, worked Saturdays and Sundays, but the local

authority had no way of dealing with us. People get fed up. 'I'm going to earn the college £10,000 to £15,000 and I get nothing back.' We spent all our time trying to work around the rules. (Assistant principal, marketing)

Other people have got it wrong

The conviction that other people needed to mend their ways and change their attitudes surfaced over and over with respondents. Colleague disapproval was often advanced as the source of all college ills: it was not FE's image that needed improvement but FE staff. The workforce had the wrong attitudes.

> No one knows what the others are doing. The employer is approached by two or three departments for work experience. They think there's no co-ordination, and they're right...The peripheral things are poor – pamphlets, the telephone: they seem like icing on the cake to the academic, but they put up barriers between the employer and the provider, and they're easy to remove, but they're not perceived as necessarily important because they're easy to remove. (College marketing officer)

Staff failed to convey enthusiasm for their offerings.

> As individuals we have to go out as ambassadors, but attitudes have to change among lecturers and support staff. If you're not happy and proud of where you work, how can you put the right image over? (College marketing officer)

The courses were inappropriate.

> You can market all you want, but the product has to be good. SCOTVEC is a product based on modules. In many cases it's not a good product. There are spelling mistakes. It's not well thought out. The module descriptions have to be fleshed out. There's no piloting. (Vice-principal, marketing)

It was the contents rather than the packaging which needed attention.

> There's no point in putting thousands of pounds into promoting cornflakes and then finding they're soggy. We have to do more than promote the service. We have to improve it. (Assistant principal, marketing)

People were college-bound and disinclined either to go out and raise money or to build profitable relationships with employers.

> What we need to do is to knock on doors more, but also seek partnerships. Think of the benefactions and subventions at Oxford University: all of us have to do this. It all improves people's estimates of us. (Principal)

> We should be working on a one-to-one basis, contacting individuals within companies. You can't use brochures to get through. (Principal)

In the midst of so much alleged ineptitude and inertia one might begin to question whether the respondents were harbouring totally unrealistic expectations about mere human beings, what they might be expected to achieve and how much they could deliver in what are (and must always remain) imperfect conditions.

Other people are not doing enough

A crucial point about such respondents was that although many were running colleges, none saw himself or herself as either responsible for current deficiencies or – more important still – capable of remedying them. Nor did anyone appear to believe that it was the job of management to change staff attitudes, stimulate enthusiasm and inspire pride in the workplace, its goods and services. Instead, external agencies were failing to deliver the requisite help.

> Some staff think selling is grubby. BTEC is helping, managing to make more of vocational qualifications and enhancing the image of college, but validating bodies could be doing more. (Assistant principal)

There was no one to look after FE.

> I went to an ACFHE and DES conference. We all felt that principals had no national body – unlike schools and the PCFC. FE is squeezed and lost in the middle. The feeling came through very strongly. We're piggy in the middle. (Principal)

The sheer indifference of an uninterested world could be overwhelming.

> We aren't well known. We have a low profile. We were ignored in the ERA publicity...I thought the DES would publicise us as a twilight zone. Our problem is that we're not experienced by the leaders of industry, like universities, but we're important for a huge

tranche of people. We're still bitty. The image is ragged...How do you describe the average technical college? You're marketing umpteen different things to umpteen different segments. (Principal)

Higher education was unsympathetic and the Government was not providing support.

A lot lies with universities and HE recognising and making clear that FE and BTEC is a good route. A lot more needs to be done at the public levels. Committees will always support BTEC, but university and polytechnic admission staff see the A level route as preferable. Art schools do the same. The Government could do a great deal, too, in promoting courses, something like what they've done in YTS and ET on television. (College marketing officer)

One respondent blamed the customers. If Government agencies could not convince indifferent employers of the need for training, what could a CFE hope to achieve?

Look at the Training Agency. Talk to officers who spend their time trying to convince industrialists that training is relevant. We tend to talk to the converted most of the time. The market which is most difficult is the small employer. (College marketing officer)

From such respondents there emerged a general mood of helplessness. This suggested that some FE 'leaders' were waiting for someone else to take charge of the troops.

Colleges need more money

A group of six respondents saw FE's image problem as capable of easy resolution through the provision of more externally provided money. This was needed to smarten up the appearance of CFEs.

A coat of paint would help. Three-quarters of classrooms are without carpets and curtains. We're doing things bit by bit, but we still have 1950s-looking furniture. (College marketing officer)

There should be a significant investment in the fabric and facilities, to attract funds to improve the physical plant. There are increasing expectations about the delivery of services among clients we weren't expecting 10 years ago. (Principal)

There's still a lot to put right – the look of the place, the classrooms, the appalling canteens. Some colleges have made a start, but others have a long way to go. (LEA marketing officer)

The sheer look of it needs to improve, the experience of moving from the front door to a room. (Principal)

Money needs to be invested in buildings and furniture to create an inviting environment. We still have huts and old amenities. (Principal)

In another college it was not unattractive appearance that was the problem but over-use of teaching facilities and inadequate social provision, both of which could be resolved only by additional funding.

We need to invest in crèches, social areas, study areas...the place is overcrowded. (Principal)

None of those who saw more resources as the answer to FE's problems touched upon where the money was to come from. The emphasis in recent years has been to reduce education spending on a per-unit basis and to force CFEs to improve their efficiency and generate ever larger proportions of their income. Even with a change of government at the next general election, it is unlikely that FE, bidding for increased funding against other public sector provision areas (schools, the infra-structure, hospitals, pensions, etc.), would come anywhere near the top of a list of priority areas, particularly if the desired funding was intended for plant refurbishment and redecoration.

Some of the above respondents were depressingly negative in their approach to improving FE's image. Even though many were managers, they seemed to regard themselves as like the driver of a hired car who has been given a dud vehicle and who blames the bumpy ride on the hire firm, its purchasing and maintenance policies and its servicing staff. If you want a smoother ride, hire a different car from a different firm.

Segmenting the market

Not all respondents share those views. Some saw the variety of FE's many markets as the source of its promotional difficulties. Only one respondent referred to ways of broadening FE's scope and range of activities.

It needs to become more flexible, get away from the school image – 36 weeks, nine to four, five days a week – and go towards 50 weeks,

Saturdays and Sundays if need be. FE should act as consultants and provide work in the workplace. It should provide for the local community. It's too narrow and restrictive. (Vice-principal)

A small group of respondents suggested that the best approach to promoting FE was to restrict its offerings, or at least market it in different ways for different groups.

> I can see range as an attraction, but most people want to know about one or two things. We need differential marketing. Maybe we need to pick horses for courses. Do you have 5,000 leaflets or do you stick to generic things? (Principal)

Differential marketing has its problems, of which not the least is cost. The mention of 5,000 leaflets is an exaggeration, but it provides an impressionistic description of the requisite task. If differentiation is required, more effort will be needed.

> If you have one open day for school leavers and another for adults, it's still not enough. With adults there are some unemployed people looking for a lifeline, and others looking for how to be proficient on a word processor in 20 hours. They're still too different a group! (Principal)

How do you market to so many distinctive segments which have so little in common? One solution is to move away from the idea of *the* or *a* college.

> Maybe we need different 'brand names' for different parts of the college. (Principal)

This respondent went on to develop the idea of a college which had a variety of product ranges, each given its own identity, run as a separate 'company' and offering its products to a distinct market, rather like the many small operations which make up the activity of a business park.

In contrast to those who wanted to expand college offerings and who thought of themselves as serving the whole community, another principal thought in terms of reducing the range of offerings, of doing less better.

> When resources are short, you need to concentrate on what you can do well. We need to offer a limited range of services of high quality. We need to get away from the idea that colleges have something for everybody. (Principal)

Getting noticed at national level

If one analyses the above respondent quotations for the kinds of actions being advocated, it becomes apparent that most of them – including those advancing the need for a national FE voice – show us people thinking primarily in terms of either transforming colleges (plant, staff, courses, investment) and/or of finding more resources for advertising and promoting CFEs. Both approaches – improving the quality of what is on offer and sending the good news to prospective customers – are valid, and both have worked for other provider groups in the past. Both are also often deployed as a two-pronged assault tactic in promotional campaigns.

The extent to which either is significantly feasible for FE in the short-term can be questioned. Dramatic college metamorphosis will take years, particularly if it is to involve large-scale replacement or retraining of staff and/or plant upgrading. The promotional goals which respondents identified are often no less ambitious. Some may be concerned only with local awareness raising, but others are much grander and involve getting information to the general public through

> ...a large national campaign with TV and cinema advertising...

> ...a national campaign, TV and the rest of it...

all of which would require vast sums of money.

Insofar as they deal with the national FE scene, these views are institution-bound, i.e. they present the outside world as seen from within the college. As such they reflect the background and professional position of the respondents, their strengths and limitations. It is significant that no one addresses either the financial or organisational aspects of the desired changes. It is even more pertinent that no one appears to see himself or herself as playing a role in the transformational process. Changing FE's image nationally is someone else's job, and presumably work which needs to be carried out by people who are not employed in colleges, where staff – including principals and marketing officers – are otherwise fully engaged.

There is a third approach at which thus far only one respondent has hinted:

> Baker's Cinderella speech was helpful even if it reinforced the image
> I'm against, but FE was at least mentioned.

In both the commercial and ideological worlds, promotional activity does not stop with improving product development and service or spending more on advertising, important as all may be. Individuals also have the potential to alter attitudes and reposition public standing, particularly if they are strategically placed and/or capable of attracting publicity. Mr Baker, as the respondent notes, did bring FE into public view, and he did so at no financial cost to CFEs, even if in the longer run FE will have to confront the deficiencies to which he drew attention.

Another interviewee took the search for 'free' publicity still further by suggesting that if FE's image is to be improved,

> We need high quality publicity. There should be videos of FE and TV commercials and a long-range soap opera on TV that could captivate millions... (Principal)

Manufacturers frequently pay cinema producers for 'product placement' opportunities in films. If the hero yearns for a particular soft drink or the heroine's cravings can be satisfied only by hamburgers from a specific international chain, business can be expected to improve. With its aura of beneficent public service, FE ought to be able to achieve product placement in national soaps without financial outlay.

According to publicity for BBC1 transmissions in March 1992, FE may get a taste of 'product placement'. 20 sketches, each of approximately two minutes in length, are planned for a single week. Each sketch 'will underline the benefit to be obtained by returning to education and training' and some at least will centre on 'going to college'. Five 15-minute documentaries are also planned for the same week of which at least one might involve a woman 'attending a local college'. One needs to say might because at the time of writing these BBC plans are under development. If they materialise as outlined in the advance publicity, it will be important for CFEs to organise themselves to respond positively to the public interest the programmes can be expected to stimulate.

A third respondent uniquely chose to pick up all these ideas and develop a conception about which others had only hinted.

> Nationally steps need to be taken at all levels to increase understanding. FE has done badly with the political lobby. Government ministers lack knowledge of FE first hand and second hand. Then we need to increase the public consciousness. At a popular level FE needs to figure in TV soaps. The Eastenders should be going to FE. In popular culture what the whole world knows about FE is Wilt, and that doesn't help us. We ought to be chatting up the scriptwriters of soaps. (Principal)

The interest here lies in the conception of FE's image problem as fundamentally political rather than attitudinal or organisational. One can deal most effectively with political problems by using political approaches. Lobbying is the tool which hundreds of groups use in Britain to bring themselves to the attention of, and to press their needs upon, key government decision makers. Television is the medium by which politicians lobby the electorate. 'Chatting up' is a form of lobbying.

What is surprising is that so few respondents should think of lobbying as a means of modifying FE's image (only one other mentioned it, and then as part of a list and without amplification). In theory, if not in practice, marketing officers spend a substantial part of their time lobbying customer suppliers such as schools and employers. On a day-to-day basis, principals spend even more of their time being lobbied by staff: for preferment, support, resources, to draw attention to needs and to ensure that particular interests are prominently spotlit in the decision maker's awareness. Principals also lobby their governors and local authorities.

Why should people whose work roles involve them in political activity at the micro level be so extraordinarily unaware of its counterpart at the macro level? The great attraction of lobbying on the national scene is that if it succeeds, for a potentially modest investment one can obtain remarkable results. Lobbyists are, after all, democracy's version of the courtier. As such, they might have been expected to appeal to the highly stratified and intensely hierarchical world of FE.

Chapter 11:
How can FE promote itself?

The picture of FE which emerges from the previous chapters is of a low-status system with a low public profile. The media tend to ignore it. Major decision makers know little about it. FE offers people a second chance, but is often regarded as second best and second rate. Like Cinderella, FE is a behind-the-scenes drudge, an unseen and unsung servant.

Unlike Cinderella, FE cannot hope to be rescued with the wave of a wand by a fairy Godparent and whisked off to prosperity and distinction. If it is to rise from the trough of public indifference, FE will have to lift itself up. It will have to take the initiative and assume responsibility. It will have to promote itself.

Is the task feasible? What can FE do to raise its profile and improve its image? Drawing upon the previous chapters, we can identify a seven point action programme.

Self help

One disheartening finding of the feasibility study interviews is the sense of helplessness which afflicts so many college principals. One gets the repeated impression that it is other people – staff, government, customers – who are to blame for what is wrong with FE. Either other people's attitudes or other people's courses. Or lack of funds. Or examination boards. Or almost anything and anyone except college management. Managing – particularly large and complex organisations – has never been easy, and no manager can hope to solve all problems, but if anything worthwhile is to be achieved, it must be management which makes it happen or takes the blame for failing.

Historically FE has had considerable inducements to pass the buck, but the situation is changing. The weakening ties between local authorities and colleges have undermined the familiar claim that it is LEA bureaucratic inflexibility which is at the root of college problems. Financial devolution is designed not merely to make colleges more cost conscious, but also to force them to take fuller control of their own destinies. If staff need developing, rooms need carpeting and attitudes need changing, it is now up to college management to find the requisite funds, difficult as that is almost certain to be. The incorporation of FE colleges can only further strengthen the college's responsibility for its own fate.

The same point can be made about FE's national image: it will not be improved through external benediction. Only FE can change its own status in the market-place. Compared to HE, FE is deficient in clout and resources. Compared to schools, FE cannot rely upon the emotional concern which surrounds the education of children. Left to their own devices, politicians cannot be expected to champion FE. There are few votes in FE.

In an ACFHE initiative which predated the feasibility study, colleges were asked to contribute a designated sum to a central fund which could be used to buy professional assistance for promoting FE. Nearly 200 colleges expressed some interest in the idea, and several dispatched cheques. Most, however, wanted further information: what would they get for their money? Why should small colleges pay as much as large colleges? How could one stop those colleges which made no contribution from benefiting from general FE promotion? No one likes free loaders.

The sum involved was £200 per year, hardly a significant investment for colleges with multi-million-pound turnovers, but apparently small enough to raise awkward questions. One is put in mind of the familiar epithet of 'penny wise and pound foolish'. Economising on inconsequential expenditure is a familiar college activity. In RCP, we worked with a college which continued to pay 19 surplus academic staff above its establishment level for a year while rationing chalk to two pieces per week per lecturer and restricting the availability of paper. In another college, all telephones were switched off for outgoing calls between 9 am and 2 pm. Such gestures stimulate the illusion of thrift, but they are financially irrelevant and usually anti-productive as well.

All professional groups have ambivalent relationships with their own kind. Individually they compete with one another, and the demise or contraction of a competitor will usually increase one's own share of the market. Collectively, however, it is in the mutual best interest of all competitors to improve their collective image. Increasing public awareness of and regard for lawyers or doctors, ambulance workers or insurance sales staff, benefits everyone who earns a living through one of these activities. One for all and all for one is a useful motto in shared adversity.

There is no way in which FE can improve its image or raise public consciousness of its activities to the exclusion of this or that individual college. Similarly, when one FE college is ignored by decision makers or treated with contempt by potential customers, it is all CFEs which are disadvantaged. In a rowboat, throwing away the oars because some crew members fail to pull their weight is not a sound idea.

Consequently, in any attempt to improve its image, FE's first problem is both to help itself and to help its own kind. This requires putting aside personal, local and political differences so that the majority of colleges can contribute to efforts designed to promote all colleges.

Finding someone to speak for FE

At the heart of the problem of self help is the essentially fragmented political nature of the FE workforce. As has already been noted, there are different professional associations for principals, vice-principals, lecturers and support staff, and several associations in some categories. There are also innumerable ad hoc FE promotional groups which spring to life from time to time, usually riding on a wave of enthusiasm emanating from a few committed individuals.

The truth of the old maxim of divide and rule is powerfully illustrated in education. Doctors and lawyers are difficult for governments to manage because they generally adopt united stances in times of difficulty. By contrast education demonstrates disunity, and FE – considering the comparative smallness of its workforce – is professionally very divided.

While fragmentation imposes constraints on the extent to which anyone can speak for a worker group, it is not necessarily fatal. A similar kind of division exists among school teachers, but organisations such as the National Union of Teachers (NUT) and the National Association of Head Teachers (NAHT) are demonstrably more effective than FE's counterparts because while FE is ignored, NUT and NAHT members are frequently used by the media as representative spokespersons. FE has thus far failed to generate any group which can act as its public representative.

NATFHE is the major lecturers' union. It has 81,000 members (both full- and part-time) and collects subscription fees of £78 per year from full-time lecturers in England, Wales and Northern Ireland (Scotland has its own union). In its London-based headquarters, NATFHE has 14 officials, and each of its 12 regional offices has one official. Of all organisations representing FE, NATFHE is best placed in terms of constituency and income to promote FE nationally. There is little evidence that it does so.

Hall (1990) describes NATFHE's function thus.

> NATFHE plays a major role in further education policy making through the representatives on most of the major examining and validating bodies, the Further Education Unit, the Further Education Staff College, the National Institute of Adult Continuing Education and so on. The Association frequently issues policy statements on major issues and newsletters. NATFHE recruits in non-university higher education, penal education departments, adult education institutes, continuing education and in training organisations. It has joint agreements with the agricultural colleges' association, the teachers of home economics, the main Scottish lecturers' union and the National Union of Teachers.

The above conveys the extent to which NATFHE is embedded in the FE system, but the phrase 'and so on' betrays more than is perhaps intended, i.e. not only a list too long for inclusion, but also a preoccupation with professional problems rather than an interest in boundary-spanning activities involving FE and its markets. Belonging to professional sub-groups has its uses, but they do not necessarily include raising public awareness.

A concern for internal college issues is certainly the impression left from a scrutiny of the 1990 issues of NATFHE's bi-monthly **NATFHE Journal**. Here one notes articles and reports on: college sexism, ageism and racism; and professional problems in general – the need for more resources, the importance of changing staff attitudes, extending access, the role of a college equal opportunities co-ordinator, dissatisfaction with BTEC, the impact of reorganisation on HE institutions, etc.

However one reacts to such material, it is difficult not to conclude that it is largely inward-looking and focused on the dissatisfactions of college life and how these might be overcome. Only occasionally does the journal look outward. One article which records proactive behaviour in response to the outside world is a two-page NATFHE survey of 19 colleges and what they are doing in preparation for 1992.

The Journal is not averse to acknowledging criticism of itself in its own pages. A questionnaire included in the January/February 1990 issue (Lanning, 1990) could potentially have been filled in by 79,000 members but produced returns from only 1,062 (1.3 per cent), which suggests either apathy or a widespread disinclination to complete and return questionnaires. of those who did respond, significant minorities complained about the political emphasis (133), dated information (134), long and poorly written articles (105), but more (282) objected to the physical presentation. What most respondents appeared to want most from the Journal was coverage of pay and conditions matters (539, 51 per cent), with education running in second place (423, 40 per cent).

NATFHE also produces **The Journal of Further and Higher Education**, which it claims 'has a reasonable number of subscribers by many academic journal standards'. Of the survey sample noted above, only 18 people (two per cent) said they were subscribers, which indicates that (like most such journals) it serves primarily small minority interests.

NATFHE's lack of activity on the national scene contrasts rather strikingly with that of the NUT. In the last quarter of 1990 there was a press campaign (noted earlier) and a national survey of teacher vacancies whose results contradicted DES findings: both were much written and talked about in the media and both helped to give school issues a prominence they might not otherwise have achieved. NATFHE is neither as large nor as wealthy as the NUT, but it has a bigger membership and a greater income than any of the other organisations which represent FE staff, so that to some extent its failure to take a leading role in promoting FE and raising public awareness of its benefits must result from disinclination rather than inability.

That this is the case is emphasised by an article by Tim Bornett in the July/August 1990 **NATFHE Journal** which argues that for NATFHE to become an effective pressure group what are required include

> more resources at national and local level relating to propaganda to include national and local advertisements ...more effective lobbying of peers, MPs, ministers, civil servants and the EEC institutions...the establishment of a professional lobbying section at Head Office, with ready and effective access to the important decision makers locally, nationally and internationally.

NATFHE may well be (Hall, 1990) 'the main trade union and professional association for staff in further education', but its national profile is distinctly low. Other FE teacher groups are even less likely to be able to represent FE, either because (Association of Agricultural Educational Staffs) they are too highly specialised or (the Further Education Lecturers National Section of the Educational Institute of Scotland) their numbers are relatively few.

Therefore, if teacher groups seem unable to promote FE nationally, where can one look for assistance? An obvious candidate might at first appear to be the Association of Principals of Colleges (APC). This is a long-standing organisation (started 1920) which acts as a professional association and trade union. APC negotiates the salaries and conditions of service of principals nationally and is represented on many national and regional bodies.

Alas, there are difficulties. APC membership hovers around 400 and can be expected to decline as the number of colleges decreases. At the moment efforts are being made to increase the annual membership fee to £150, but even this sum cannot result in resources sufficient to impact on FE's national image. As is so frequent in education, APC has to rely for continuity on a part-time secretary and the intermittent assistance of practising principals.

One continuing dilemma for APC is whether to opt for exclusivity (principals only), which keeps it small and poor, or to seek to recruit all college managers, which could extend its power base and increase its resources. APC's choice is reflected in other comparable small organisations. For vice-principals there is the Association of Vice-Principals of Colleges (AVPC). Registrars and Chief Administrative Officers (CAOs) have the Association of College Registrars and Administrators (ACRA). Until fairly recently, other kinds of college managers had no specific organisations of their own.

In an attempt to confront the problem, in 1987 APC was involved in establishing the Association for College Management (ACM) intended to attract all college senior management, registered as a trades union but 'first and foremost a professional association which concerns itself with the development of professionalism amongst college managers'. In mid-1990 ACM had 2,000 members and claimed in its promotional literature all the apparent benefits of wide membership.

> Its unique membership structure embraces all members of the college management team. This enables it to exert informed pressure on policy makers and places it in the position of being the only organisation speaking for, and representing, the views and interests of all managers in further and higher education.

The ACM also claims to be 'increasing the professional and public awareness of ACM and its role in the education service' by increasing membership 'on all bodies which affect members' interests' and by publishing its own views. With a membership fee of only £30 (soon to be raised), ACM is unlikely, however, to become wealthy. Moreover, members of APC are 'automatically members of ACM', which further reduces the available funds.

More recently APC has become absorbed with changes imposed by devolved financial responsibility. If principals are now performing as chief executives – negotiating their own salaries and conditions of service as well as those of other staff on the management salaries spine – does this not impose the necessity for separateness from other managers? Apparently yes, for APC's Council in September 1990 passed a resolution recommending the future independence of APC outside ACM.

Somewhere between APC with its exclusivity and ACM with its broad membership is the Association of Colleges for Further and Higher Education (ACFHE). Membership of ACFHE (350 FE colleges at present) enables a college to

> ...nominate in writing three representatives who shall include the chairman or other member of the governing body and the principal.

Therefore, individual representation is currently limited to three times the number of colleges, which might be seen as a restriction, but which has enabled ACFHE to claim that through its governing body membership it represents the interests not merely of managers but also of college staff and students, employers and LEAs, as well as other users of college services. ACFHE membership fees are currently based on the college's number of full-time-equivalent (FTE) students: £75 for 0 – 2,000 FTE students; £85 for 2,001 – 4,000; £100 for 4,001 and over. (Proposals for a radically altered scale are discussed below.)

In recent years, ACFHE has maintained a higher profile than some of its competitors. In 1989, with financial support from The Staff College and DES, ACFHE promoted a feasibility study into the viability of an FE Marketing Unit. This led to a DES grant-in-aid of £200,000 for the Unit, which is being housed for the immediate future at The Staff College.

The Unit is intended to sell marketing goods and services to FE colleges and in the process to generate sufficient profits to pay for the promotion of FE at national level. The expectation is that by acting as broker and negotiating bulk purchases, the Unit should be able to offer its services at competitive prices, while still maintaining an acceptable profit margin. Whether it can achieve this remains to be seen.

In theory, the close relationship between ACFHE and the Unit – with ACFHE as the dominant member of the Unit's steering committee during the initial two-year project stage – should lead to ACFHE's involvement in the intended FE promotional activity, with the Unit as a kind of associated 'company' devoted to income generation. This eventuality, of course, is some way off. At the time of writing, the Unit has been trading for only a few months. In the meantime, difficulties remain.

Firstly there is the irony that APC, AVPC, ACM and ACFHE do not necessarily represent distinctive strands of the FE service, since members of one organisation can also belong to one or two others (not to mention NATFHE and EIS). From time to time still more groups emerge. There is the Tertiary Colleges Association (TCA) which has begun to lobby for member interests. It has recently decided to widen its membership so as to include people who are not employed in tertiary colleges but who are in sympathy with TCA aims. There is a ginger group, the FE Campaign Group, which calls itself 'a new voice for further education'. And so on...

What we have is overlapping membership involving people who wear a variety of different hats to represent different aspects of their professional roles. If the public is confused by – or simply oblivious to – so much diversity involving so few people, this is hardly surprising. Nor is it beneficial to FE.

Secondly, and more important, the result of so many groups representing so many nuances of organisational and political differentiation is a superabundance of small organisations, each poorly funded and run by part-time organisers assisted by part-time secretaries. What FE requires is a professional body comparable to the CBI with a full-time secretariat and a policy agenda designed to promote the interests of the service and to raise its profile.

The model for an FE promotional body

Leaving aside the still-evolving ACFHE-Marketing Unit relationship, we might postulate how an FE promotional body would ideally look. To start with, while it could encompass FE's plurality within its internal committee and sub-group structures, its public face would need to reflect widespread unity. In the media, spokespersons do not necessarily speak for every one, but they do represent everyone. They are there to draw public attention to their constituents and to put their interests on the agenda.

Moreover, the body's mission would have to be discharged not from the regions but from the centre. Such a commitment would in turn require full-time professionals rather than the traditional part-timers who try to work gratis at a large and complex task in the interstices between other paid commitments. The body would need to be London-based, because in Britain (for better or worse) the capital is the decision making centre of the country.

A promotional FE body would require funding, and there is no chance of this emerging from anywhere other than FE itself. That means thinking in terms of something more than £35 here and £75 there. A £2 billion industry ought to be able to afford five or 10 full-time people to promote its interests. In turn, the professional body should be able to generate some part of its requisite income. Even if the Marketing Unit eventually makes a contribution towards the cause, FE colleges themselves cannot hope to have their interests represented by a professional body without also reaching into their devolved or incorporated pockets. If no one thus far speaks for FE, only FE can change the situation.

There exists an overseas model which FE would do well to consider, the American Association of Community and Junior Colleges (AACJC). This organisation was started in 1920 when there were only 207 two-year institutions. Now, when there are 1,200 community, technical and junior colleges, AACJC boasts membership of more than 90 per cent of all public colleges and over one-third of independent two-year colleges.

Instead of encouraging members with special interests to cut themselves off in separate organisations, AACJC brings them all under one umbrella. The Presidents Academy provides in-service education and professional development activities for chief executives. The Professional Administrators Development Institute runs workshops for all administrators. Commissions have been established by the AACJC Board of Directors to provide advice on targeted areas such as improving minority education, the problems of small/rural community colleges, international satellite working, etc.

Even more interesting from our point of view, AACJC has joined with the Association of Community College Trustees (trustees are the equivalent of our college governors) to create the Joint Commission on Federal Relations. This is based in Washington DC and monitors federal legislation and regulations, promoting those which best serve the interests of members. Each year, the Association also identifies priority areas and issues a public policy agenda.

AACJC is affiliated to a large number of independent bodies representing a wide range of interests (e.g. women, Hispanic, research, Black American) and runs three special-focus consortia with membership open to institutions and individuals. It numbers major US firms (e.g. General Motors Corporation, Ford Motor Company, IBM Corporation, WK Kellogg Foundation) and government agencies (e.g. Department of Commerce, Department of Defense, Department of Education) among its support groups, who fund special projects and general Association activities.

AACJC's journal for 1990 has provided articles on how community colleges can assist employers with the 'on-going critical need for workers with higher levels of technical and problem-solving skills'; a programme which allows colleges to draw upon teaching inputs from nationally prominent speakers through the use of live satellite video teleconference arrangements; and problems of employee retention. In 1989 the Association collected $1,250,000 in fees and returned 24 per cent to member colleges through project mini-grants.

To use an American expression, US community, technical and junior colleges have 'got their act together'. FE has not.

Current efforts to create a promotional body

An indication that at least some of FE is aware of its promotional deficiencies is suggested by current (mid-1991) efforts to set up a 'New ACFHE', a move stimulated by the likelihood of corporate status. The model is the AACJC, which ACFHE Council members have visited in the US. What is proposed is a dramatic overhaul of ACFHE and the establishment of a quite different organisation.

A prospectus for the proposed organisation prints a policy agenda adopted at the 1991 annual general meeting of which the principles include:

- colleges need a strong unified and convincing voice in education and training circles. The Association should work for a consensus among its members and act as an advocate for institutions and their governing bodies;

- colleges are different from each other in purpose and character. The Association should promote respect for the individuality of institutions within its overall advocacy for the sector;

- the specialist functions of further education are encouraged and supported by a number of national organisations. The Association should forge links and undertake activities with other appropriate bodies to carry its own agenda forward.

The first is clearly the most significant. The second and third acknowledge the political difficulties FE faces in getting its act together. A 'takeover bid' is what most small competitors fear: ACFHE's task involves not merely raising the necessary resources for its ambitious undertaking (discussed below) but winning the co-operation of non-ACFHE members if the new organisation is to be able to describe itself as representative of a fragmented service.

In order to achieve its goals, ACFHE acknowledges a need

> ...to establish a professional staff, secretariat and permanent office. While keeping its organisation as slim as possible...ACFHE needs to raise approximately £250,000 annually.

> In the first instance this sum will need to come mainly from college subscriptions. However, once a chief executive and supporting staff are in post, the Association will also seek substantial commercial sponsorship and will raise revenue from conferences and other trading activities.

The means is a membership subscription system related to 'ability to pay', involving seven categories of colleges based on full-time-equivalent student numbers – from 'up to 400' to 'above 5,700' – and ranging from £100 to £2,000 per college per year. The starting date is January 1992. The key questions which remain to be answered are whether the colleges will find the new scales acceptable and whether, if they do, the resulting sum will be sufficient to establish the 'new' ACFHE.

Learning to target market segments

The kind of diversity which the ACFHE initiative discussed above acknowledges for political reasons – 'respect for the individuality of institutions' – is only one kind of plurality problem which afflicts FE.

One of the many advantages enjoyed by AACJC is that it represents in the public eye a fairly well defined product, the college which follows on from school and can represent the first part of an undergraduate course. FE is less tidy: it overlaps with schools, runs programmes which are peculiar to its own kind, and includes HE.

In one way the latter has decreased since 89 major HE institutions received corporate status, taking large-scale HE work away from various kinds of hybrid FE-HE colleges, but also leaving some FE colleges with an HE 'residue' in institutions whose HE work was insufficient for achieving corporate status. Paradoxically, HE has since begun to make new inroads into FE colleges, because some corporate HE establishments have begun franchising undergraduate work to

FE colleges, thus bringing the latter closer to the US junior college model. [Parenthetically one might note a further movement towards franchising 'downwards' into schools, which means that we are likely to end up not with more streamlined FE or school systems, but with increased diversity.]

An uncomfortable consequence is that agencies such as APC, ACM, AVPC and ACFHE cover both FE (the majority) and HE (the minority). If FE's agencies were to exclude HE, they would undoubtedly lose members and income, while reducing their sphere of influence. They would also be cutting themselves off from what, in the academic pecking order, represents enhanced status. CFE managers may bemoan the difficulty of marketing such plurality, but few are seeking to abandon HE and many are actively exploring ways of obtaining the franchise for local undergraduate work.

One might summarise what is required for effective FE promotion as follows.

1. There is a need to conceptualise the market in terms of distinct segments, e.g. women returners, 16+ school leavers, leisure education.

2. FE should be thinking in terms of distinct campaigns, one or possibly two per year in the first instance, organised to cover all the component FE (and even HE) areas over a limited number of years, i.e. everyone gets a turn, but not at the same time.

3. For each promotional campaign, FE ought to seek external sponsorship. For example, in the case of women returners, FE should be looking for assistance from the Equal Opportunities Commission and all of the leading women's groups, as well as raising additional funding from other agencies and business groups eager to be associated with the activity in hand. The latter may well necessitate joint initiatives with joint logos, or linked displays and presentations.

4. In order to facilitate the work identified in 3 above, FE ought to affiliate on a permanent basis with agencies which share its interests in particular customer groups. The purpose here is to know whether, for example, BTEC is targeting the 18+ market in June 1993 and promoting awareness that its awards offer advanced entry into first degrees. Affiliation should enable FE to identify relatively early where it might join with others to promote a common goal and to be actively involved in all planning stages.

5. FE promotional campaigns should involve the co-ordination of activity at national level with linked local initiatives. Taking women returners as an example again, efforts should be made at a national level for television programmes (chat shows, documentaries, film seasons), journalism (features in the press and women's magazines), conferences and events involving well known personalities to coincide with related activity at local level, so that potential customers are being contacted at as many points as possible, i.e. you saw it on television, you can buy it here.

6. To enable colleges to play their campaign role at a local level, suitable promotional materials (e.g. videos, radio/TV/cinema advertisements, posters, leaflets) should be made available for purchase by colleges.

There are two problems with such a promotional strategy. Firstly it requires central organisation, a professional body with full-time staff who can co-ordinate and integrate, make contacts, seek sponsors, build networks. At the moment FE has no such body. Secondly, forward planning is vital if national and local initiatives are to coincide, and FE has a long history of short-term planning at best.

Raising FE's profile

Campaigns have their uses, but FE has a problem which they cannot easily resolve: in terms of clout and prominence it is positioned at the margins of the educational world. Too few know about it and even fewer care about it. If that is to change, FE needs to raise public awareness of its activities and the opportunities it provides, and it needs to direct its efforts at the national rather than the local level.

In one way, FE has a model for what is required in that many colleges have already set up arrangements for feeding interesting material to the local press, but in another way the process is a kind of double-edged sword. Very few local papers are associated with high quality in terms of layout, printing, art work, writing or accuracy. They represent the bottom end of the market, and FE may impact by that means, but it also becomes identified with the second best and the second rate, especially since it generally appears only in the local press. There is a consequent need for FE to make comparable efforts at the national level. The surveys of national media discussed above have made abundantly clear that there is a gap waiting to be filled. FE's task is to enable others to perceive the gap as well, and to help them to fill it. The financial collapse of a high profile college should not be the only kind of FE news that interests the quality press.

No less important is for FE to take up the suggestion put by several of the feasibility study respondents, that it should lobby television soap scriptwriters to work an FE connection into their scripts. The material is potentially fascinating in any number of ways. FE staff are living in a period of rapid and wide-ranging change. Some are in or are moving on to second careers and/or have the added interest of varied external activities. Young FE students study and train, fall in and out of love, and go on to make careers for themselves – as students do everywhere – so that anyone looking for an educational setting could turn as easily to FE as to HE or schools.

There is the additional attraction that FE covers the widest imaginable curriculum range, from art to bricklaying, management to engineering, laboratory to classroom study, which suggests there are distinctive advantages as far as variety of setting is concerned.

Rather more unusually, FE also involves people of all ages from all walks of life and socio-economic backgrounds pursuing all kinds of activities. Outside the classroom, FE has its share of organisational politics, intrigue and manoeuvring. Perhaps the incorporated college with its new-style chief executive principal may lead to a situation in which (academic) boardroom drama takes on features usually associated with the commercial world. There is, of course, always a danger in bringing a whiff of real life into the depiction of educational activity, but there is also scope for humanising it and enhancing public perceptions of the area.

The current emphasis on retraining and the growing need for members of the workforce to acquire new skills and pursue new career directions lends itself to biographical series treatment in both newspapers and television documentaries, as the projected 1992 BBC1 campaign for adult returners indicates. Increasingly FE is and will be linking with Continental colleges as a 1992-focused overseas component becomes a required part of more and more FE courses. Scriptwriters and journalists also have the advantage of dealing with a setting which is a mixture of the familiar, because of the millions of people who have attended FE classes, and the unknown, because of neglect by the media.

In order for the national media to turn their attention to FE, the service itself has to take a proactive role, making contacts, setting up networks, working creatively to convince others of the advantages inherent in raising FE's profile. The goal ought to be not merely to get noticed in occasional features and programmes but to have the FE view sought as a matter of course whenever appropriate educational issues are raised. Because industry and private trainers have in the past decade been progressively more and more identified with training to the exclusion of CFEs, the latter should be progressively working themselves into the centre of the training map.

Yet again, that points to the need for a central agency, part of whose promotional brief is to ensure that the newspapers and journals discussed in an earlier chapter pay attention not merely to schools and HE, but to FE as well. Such an agency ought also to be acting as a link between the media and CFEs, as a reference point for reporters who are looking for someone to interview and directors who want a college in which they can film.

Developing a quality service

Effective promotion is not solely a matter of convincing people that you have what they need and want, but also of being able to deliver what they have been encouraged to believe you can offer. If the public image of FE is of the dowdy, using advertisements and videos to suggest vitality, brightness and dynamism will be counterproductive if the reality leaves people feeling that they have been conned. FE must both promote itself better and make itself worthy of promotion.

Most of British FE is at best 1960s stock, inexpensive public building erected to a standard which has since been superseded in public expectation. Compared to the best US, Continental and Australian colleges, British CFEs are usually much worse, and poorly equipped. Resourcing cuts over the past 15 years have tended to drive maintenance and repairs to the bottom of the priorities list, so that many colleges – like schools – are in need of massive investment for improvement. It is highly unlikely that FE is going to be helped to overcome its deficiencies except through its own efforts.

In practical terms, colleges need to clean up their buildings; develop attractive entrance areas; resurface their car parks (if they have any); signpost visitors clearly; and create attractive environments at the major points of initial customer contact, attractive, that is, to at least the same degree as the principals' study and the governing body meeting room. CFEs also require repainting and refurbishing, carpeting and landscaping.

In many colleges, customer care still awaits development, both in terms of physical plant (furniture, equipment, lighting) and staff (more and better trained). That means that there is a need for better telephone and reception services, but also for more effective personal and academic counselling and for job placement services. Getting customers to the attractive college and making them welcome are first steps. Later there is a requirement for assisting them to find and survive the right courses and for ensuring that they are helped to locate the right kind of more advanced courses and/or employment if they are not already in jobs they wish to retain.

The current emphasis upon quality – through BS 5750 and the total quality management (TQM) movement – requires colleges to turn their attention more and more to the customer perspective, since it is the customer who in a service industry is the final arbiter of quality. There is thus a need to involve customers as students more fully and centrally in course delivery. In turn, that means surveying students about their perceptions of the college and its courses and using the resulting data to make requisite improvements, a procedure which has been routine in North American colleges for decades but which can still strike fear in the hearts of many CFE staff.

There is a need, too, for staff appraisal procedures (only recently agreed as part of the 1991 pay settlement) which involve assessment of teaching itself, instead of the compromise of the appraisal interview held in a manager's office and conducted without the benefit of any kind of data beyond uncorroborated teacher impressions.

Quality approaches such as TQM require the involvement of all staff, a shift in emphasis which must inevitably reach the heart of the social class divide which is so clearly visible in the gulf between teaching and support staff in most CFEs. Quality is thus not solely a matter of better decor and a welcoming smile, but necessitates a massive cultural transformation as well.

It is one thing to make lists of obvious deficiencies and another to effect remedies. The college dilemma is that as resources have become scarcer so the list of necessary improvements has grown longer. There is now both more to do and less to do it with.

One is inclined to stress that widespread major improvements will take years or even decades, except that few colleges can afford to delay action. The general expectation is that the FE system will contract and jobs will be lost. Partly this will result from rationalisation for demographic reasons, but it will also derive from pressure for greater productivity and from the effects of increased competition – from schools, other colleges, the private sector, and employers, particularly if training credits are adopted.

The more proactive colleges have begun to take steps and establish new bench marks: improved reception areas, cleaned up corridors, carpeted rooms, effective attempts at signposting, in-service courses in customer care. If our food, homes, clothing, technology, appliances and life expectations are all improving, colleges cannot afford to stand still or to excuse inaction through lack of funding. They certainly need money, but they will have to earn it instead of waiting for someone else to give it to them.

Lobbying decision makers

At the time when the Education Reform Bill was going through Parliament, there was a general perception among FE observers that the focus was on schools and HE, with FE pushed to the fringes until it was out of view. The explanation was that the nation's decision makers – as usual – were displaying their ignorance of FE, i.e. it was other people, not FE, who were at fault. The truth is that decision makers are not obliged to worry about FE unless FE convinces them that failing to do so is disadvantageous.

In the example of the AACJC noted above, the Association maintains a presence in Washington DC not merely to monitor federal legislation and regulations in order to obtain information, but also to bring pressure on those who produce the legislation and regulations to ensure that the results protect and promote the interests of the Association's members as fully as possible. The AACJC lobbies the US government.

In Britain lobbying involves pressuring Members of the two Houses of Parliament, politicians and their advisers, and government officials. Its practice has grown dramatically since the end of the Second World War and now extends to the European Parliament as well. Some people regard lobbying as improper, as a form of clandestine political manoeuvring. Others (Davies, 1985) argue that lobbying is a part of the democratic process and has distinct advantages: political monitoring, informing, protecting minorities, sustaining debate, mobilising and countervailing.

Lobbying is undertaken by pressure groups, trade unions and concerned individuals from what they would claim are non-commercial motives, i.e. to serve ideological or political ends (Dubs, 1988). One justification for the activity is that the real opposition to government and powerful interests exists not in Her Majesty's Official Opposition in Parliament but in the pressure groups outside, and lobbying is therefore an intrinsic component of the democratic process. It is also important to note that (Miller, 1987)

> At least 100 MPs and an indeterminate number of Peers (since the latter do not have to register their interests) are retained by organisations to provide them with advice; to act as spokesmen for their interests or to assist them with obtaining access to other MPs, Peers and Ministers.

There is also commercial lobbying activity. Some business interests such as firms and trade associations employ lobbyists to work for them in-house as members of their staffs, while others purchase the services of lobbying firms or public affairs consultants. All the indicators suggest that lobbying is growing rather than declining and that more and more groups will turn to lobbying as they perceive the disadvantages of not lobbying. There is an increasing body of literature on lobbying, what to do and not do, techniques and tactics, using MPs to obtain publicity, etc.

As was noted in the previous chapter, only two feasibility study respondents recommended lobbying as a means of promoting FE. The tendency to ignore lobbying does not mean that no individuals have ever approached MPs or officials. The TCA has for some time been lobbying MPs. Prior to Mr Clarke's March announcement, groups of principals were busy lobbying for FE corporate status, 'pleading to be free from local shackles' as the TES (1991a) put it.

Such efforts, however, have traditionally been ad hoc, intermittent and unco-ordinated across the service. If FE is to promote itself nationally it will have to embrace lobbying as a central part of its promotional strategy and co-ordinate its efforts (both nationally and locally) on behalf of the FE industry as a whole.

If FE comes to take its promotional interests seriously and accepts the necessity for regular and systematic lobbying, it will have to move from the notion of occasional lobbying activity by enthusiastic college principals to something more professional. That would require either employing a commercial lobbying firm or getting some member or members of the full-time staff of its professional body to undertake the task. In either case, FE needs to accept the challenge of a proactive promotional stance, which is in essence what lobbying is.

Adopting a positive approach

The reader may feel that many of the criticisms of FE advanced in this and previous chapters are unduly negative and therefore unfair, but a scrutiny of the feasibility study responses will show that when it comes to knocking FE no one does it better than those who work in it. FE is an industry with a deep rooted inferiority complex which manifests itself most conspicuously in the belief that HE is best and FE is second best.

For years the conviction has been buttressed by course grading and resourcing systems which ensured that higher retained its ascendancy by paying higher more. One of the many differences waiting to be grasped in devolved financial control and its attendant business ethic is that in the market-place the old value system does not necessarily hold. An outstanding French language teacher can command £500 or £600 a day to deliver a crash course to a sales team, a much higher price tag than might be applied to a distinguished professor whose specialism is the drama of Racine or the operas of Lully. Many of the inherited values which FE has tended to support are being challenged in the rapidly changing outside world.

Among marketeers, it is generally agreed that it is easiest to market products which represent a unique selling proposition (USP), i.e. offer benefits which cannot be obtained elsewhere. FE's deference towards HE often surfaces in attempts to sell itself as a stepping-stone to HE and in the greater respect (and resources) it accords to those college sections which offer HE courses. If FE is to gain public recognition as a valuable service in its own right, it will have to take pride in what differentiates itself from others, instead of extolling only those features in which it resembles its competitors.

FE's USP is that it offers a bridge between the world of study and the world of work, and a bridge across which people can travel repeatedly in both directions over an entire adult lifetime. Its closeness to the workplace and its remoteness from academe need to be perceived as strengths rather than as disadvantages. It is the abiding misfortune of so much of British education that provider institutions constantly strive to mimic what they are not – state schools seeking to turn themselves into public schools, polytechnics longing to be universities – instead of valuing what they are. In so doing they ensure that their own negative self-image is perceived and accepted within the market-place.

The justification for urging colleges to smarten up their buildings is thus not only that customers are more likely to be attracted by improved decor, but also that the immediate physical impression which anyone makes is an indicator of both how one views oneself and how one views others. The imminent arrival of important visitors encourages most of us to clear up, tidy up, clean up and wash up. In respecting others, we express our own self-respect.

The most effective promotion is based on conviction and confidence. If FE colleges do not believe in themselves and like themselves, why should anyone else?

Appendix A:
The feasibility study national survey

The national survey referred to in this book was conducted in autumn 1989 as part of a feasibility study designed to gauge college support for a Further Education Marketing Unit. There were 62 respondents – principals, vice-principals, LEA and college marketing officers employed in 50 colleges and two LEAs – from England, Scotland and Wales.

The respondents formed two groups of 31 each.

- An opportunity sample of Marketing Network members (14) attending a FESC conference and of staff (17) working in colleges to which access could be easily obtained, all interviewed face to face; and

- people drawn randomly from the ACFHE list of members interested in supporting an FE promotional unit and interviewed over the telephone.

In both instances the same instrument was used and there were no significant differences in responses from the two groups. Ten respondents represented second or third opinions from one of the 50 colleges, at which point it was apparent that one ought (not surprisingly) to expect divergent views within the same institution.

The 50 colleges involved encompassed substantial variety within the most significant variables: size (in terms of FTE students), geographical spread, urban/ rural sites, level (further/higher education) and range (mono/polytechnic) of work. In the event equal numbers had and did not have college marketing units, a useful means of distinguishing between those openly committed to marketing and those whose marketing work is less advanced.

Respondents were asked the following questions.

1. Does your college have a marketing unit?

2. If so, how many staff does it employ?

3. Do you have a marketing budget?

4. What image do you think FE has among individual customers – potential students (and their parents)?

5. What image do you think FE has among employers?

6. How would you like to see FE's image changed, if at all?

7. What (if anything) do you think could/should be done to improve FE's image?

Respondents were drawn from the following organisations.

Colleges

Anniesland College, Glasgow
Barmulloch College, Glasgow
Bournemouth & Poole College of FE
Bournville College of FE
Brooklands Technical College
Brooklyn College
Cauldon College
Central College of Commerce, Glasgow
Clydebank College, Clydebank
Cricklands College
Croydon College
Dacorum College
East Devon College
Glasgow College of Food Technology
Greenhill College
Hall Green College
Harringey College
Havering Technical College
Henley College
James Watt College, Greenock
Kingsway College
Lancashire and Morecambe College
Melton Mowbray College of FE
Mid-Glamorgan College of Agriculture and Horticulture
Milton Keynes College
New College Durham
Newcastle College of FE
Newham Community College
North Cheshire College
North East Surrey College of Technology

North East Worcestershire College
North Manchester Community College
North Warwickshire College of Technology and Art
Oxford College of FE
Reid Kerr College, Paisley
Rhondda College
Rockingham College of FE
St Helen's College
Salford College of FE
South Mersey College
South Nottinghamshire College of FE
Southampton College
Stevenson College, Edinburgh
Stow College, Glasgow
Swindon College
Thurrock Technical College
Wellingborough College
Willesden College of Technology
Windsor and Maidenhead College
Ystrad Mynach College of FE

Local education authorities

Lancashire
Wiltshire

Appendix B:
College prospectuses

In the last week of May 1990 staff in the Further Education Staff College (now The Staff College) library wrote to all UK public-sector colleges requesting their current prospectuses by return post for research and archival use. By 20th July (the last day on which a research assistant was available) 95 FE propectuses had arrived and these were included in the survey. They are listed below.

It would have been tidy to have taken prospectuses from the same academic session, but for a variety of reasons that proved impossible. Some colleges have taken to producing general prospectuses which can be used for several years, thus saving on production and printing costs. Upon occasion this has led to a two-year designation (e.g. 1989-91) but more often it has resulted in the omission of any date. One college pasted a new date over the old one. The majority of prospectuses which can be dated derive from 1990-91, but some colleges now choose to use the calendar year (e.g. 1990). A few prospectuses derive from either 1989-90 (where later ones were not available) or 1991-92 (where forward planning had yielded exceptionally early results).

Abingdon College
Angus College of FE
Anniesland College
Antrim Technical College
Banff and Buchan College of FE
Barnet College
Barnfield College
Basildon College of FE
Basingstoke Technical College
Bell College of Technology
Beverley College of FE
Bishop Auckland Technical College
Blackpool and The Fylde College
Bracknell College

Bradford and Ilkley Community College
Bridgnorth and South Shropshire College
Brooklands College
Buckinghamshire College
Burton-upon-Trent Technical College
Cardonald College
Carshalton College
Chichester College of Technology
Colchester Institute
Coleg Glan Hafren
Coleraine Technical College
Coventry Technical College
Croydon College
Dartington College of Arts

Derwentside College
Dumfries and Galloway College of Technology
Dundee Institute of Technology
Eastbourne College of Arts and Technology
Ebbw Vale College of FE
Fareham Tertiary College
Halesowen College
Harrogate College
Hastings College of Arts and Technology
Hendon College of FE
Herefordshire Technical College
Hereward College of FE
Hinckley College of FE
Hounslow Borough College
Huddersfield Technical College
Huntingdonshire College
Isle of Wight College of Arts and Technology
Jewel and Esk College
Keighley Technical College
Kingston College of FE
Lancaster and Morecambe College
Langside College
Leek College of FE and School of Art
Lewes Tertiary College
Loughborough College
Macclesfield College of FE
Melton Mowbray College of FE
Millbrook College
Motherwell College
Newark College
Newham Community College
Newport College of FE
Norfolk Institute of Art and Design
North Devon College

North Lindsey College of Technology
North London College
North Oxfordshire Technical College and School of Art
North Warwickshire College of Technology and Art
North West College of Technology
North West Kent College of Technology
Northampton College of FE
Orpington College of FE
Park Lane College
People's College of FE
Peterlee College
Redbridge Technical College
Salisbury College of Technology
School of Art and Design Portsmouth
Scottish College of Textiles
South Manchester Community College
South Nottinghamshire College of FE
Southport College of Arts and Technology
Stoke on Trent College
Strode College
Thames Valley College
Thurso Technical College
Uxbridge College
Wakefield District College
Walsall College of Technology
Waltham Forest College
Wellingborough College
West Dean College
Willesden College of Technology
Winchester College of Art
Wirral Metropolitan College
Woolwich College
York College of Arts and Technology

Appendix C:
Colleges and local newspapers

Although FE colleges sometimes offer courses which aim to recruit nationally, the majority of provision is intended for local residents, for which reason most college newspaper advertising appears in local papers. It therefore seemed appropriate to investigate a) how colleges promoted themselves in local newspapers, and b) how local newspapers reported college activity.

The scale of the operation was potentially overwhelming and quite beyond the limits of the available resources. Growth in the number of newspapers has been particularly prolific following recent printing technology advances, and this increase is reflected in the available statistics (Willings Press Guide, 1990, published by Reed Information Services). In 1989 there were 124 daily newspapers and in 1990, 136; for corresponding years 20 and 30 Sunday newspapers and 1,553 and 2,020 Greater London, county and local newspapers, altogether a rise from 1,697 to 2,186 outlets, representing an increase of nearly 29 per cent.

In the event I randomly selected three dozen papers from the Willings list, seeking to include northern and southern England, Scotland and Wales, daily and weekly papers with varied circulations (from 15,000 to 650,000). All one could hope for was a 'flavour' of how FE is presented to the general public, and the resulting data could not be said to be either comprehensive or to possess any statistical validity. Nor would any one newspaper necessarily reveal whether the local college advertised or was written about, since in some areas there were two or more papers available.

In the four weeks from 20 August to 17 September – the last two weeks in the first month and the first two in the second – copies of the newspapers listed below were either requested or bought, depending on whether they were distributed free or sold. The mailing systems of many newspapers were clearly taxed by the requirement to post copies to a Blagdon address. In some instances (e.g. the Comet Leaders) it could not have been worth the publisher's while to provide more than a sample, which might explain why only one copy arrived from Bexley, Bromley, Caterham, Croydon and Orpington. In others (e.g. Basingstoke Gazette, Scunthorpe

Target, Edinburgh Herald and Post) copies continued to arrive after the cut-off date. One daily (Glasgow Herald) sent 23 issues. In the event, it was decided to use everything that had arrived (202 papers).

It was expected that this period would coincide with the main FE autumn enrolment days across the country and as a result ought to reveal both FE advertising and FE itself as the newsworthy focus of local interest. The newspapers consulted are listed with circulation statistics from Willings; those marked with an * (55 per cent of the total) contained material on FE.

	Newspaper	Circulation	Copies
*	Barnet Borough Times	24,000	4
*	Barrow and West Cumberland Advertiser	51,313	4
*	Basingstoke Gazette	14,395	5
*	Bedford Herald and Post	54,820	4
	Bexley and Eltham Comet Leader	93,890	1
*	Bradford Star	116,711	3
*	Brighton and Hove Leader	141,578	4
	Bromley Comet Leader	102,261	1
	Caterham Comet Leader	650,000	1
	Croydon Comet Leader	99,986	1
*	Derby Express	25,013	4
*	Dundee Extra	74,000	4
*	Edinburgh Herald and Post	220,950	5
	Edinburgh and Lothians Post	221,205	1
*	Enfield Advertiser	101,021	2
*	Essex Chronical	36,821	4
*	Finchley Advertiser	41,915	3
*	Glasgow Herald	124,725	24
	Hammersmith and Fulham Guardian	30,000	4
*	Haringey Advertiser	62,361	3
*	Leicester Mail	120,783	4
*	Liverpool Echo	207,013	24
	Milton Keynes Mirror	85,653	2
	North Kent Courier	150,000	2
	Orpington & District Comet Leader	54,988	1
	Oxford Star	125,586	4
	Penzance, St Ives & Hayle Leader	18,360	2
*	Poole and Dorset Advertiser	56,303	5

	St Helens Star	78,144	5
*	Scunthorpe Target	54,056	6
*	Shropshire Star	100,008	24
*	Somerset Express	152,384	4
	Streatham Guardian	67,868	4
	Teeside Times	183,996	5
	Waltham Forest Express	82,262	4
	Western Mail	77,830	24
	Total		**202**

Appendix D: Acronyms

Acronyms and initialisms represent part of the professional code through which educationists/trainers communicate. For the uninitiated, or the forgetful, the following is offered, with apologies for what is (to some) obvious.

AACJC	American Association of Community and Junior Colleges
ACFHE	Association of Colleges for Further and Higher Education
ACM	Association for College Management
ACRA	Association of College Registrars and Administrators
AE	Adult education
AFE	Advanced further eduction
A level	Advanced Level of the General Certificate of Education
ALH	Average (weekly) lecturer (class contact) hours
APC	Association of Principals of Colleges
ASH	Average (weekly) student taught hours
AVPC	Association of Vice-Principals of Colleges
BS	British Standard
BTEC	Business and Technology Education Council
CAD	Computer aided design
CAM	Computer aided manufacture
CAO	Chief administrative officer
CBI	Confederation of British Industry
CDP	Committee of Directors of Polytechnics
CEO	Chief education officer
CFE	College of further education
CNAA	Council for National Academic Awards

DE	Department of Employment
DES	Department of Education and Science
EIS	Educational Institute of Scotland
EMIE	Education Management Information Exchange
ERA	Education Reform Act
ET	Employment training
FE	Further education
FESC	Further Education Staff College (now The Staff College)
FEU	Further Education Unit
FTE	Full-time equivalent
GCE	General Certificate of Education
HE	Higher education
H-Grade	Higher Grade of the Scottish Certificate of Education
HMSO	Her Majesty's Stationery Office
LA	Local authority
LEA	Local education authority
LEC	Local Enterprise Companies
LMC	Local management of colleges
LMS	Local management of schools
MBA	Master of Business Administration
MP	Member of Parliament
MPhil	Master of Philosophy Degree
MSC	Manpower Services Commission
NALGO	National and Local Government Officers Association
NAFE	Non-Advanced Further Education
NAHT	National Association of Head Teachers
NATFHE	National Association of Teachers in Further and Higher Education
NEBSS	National Examinations Board for Supervisory Studies
NEDO	National Economic Development Office
NFER	National Foundation for Educational Research
NUT	National Union of Teachers

NVQ	National Vocational Qualification
PBOG	Polytechnic Building Officers Group
PCFC	Polytechnics and Colleges Funding Council
PEL	Paid educational leave
PETRA	Programme for the Vocational Training and Preparation of Young People
PhD	Doctor of Philosophy Degree
PICKUP	Professional Industrial and Commercial Updating (courses for employed adults)
PIN	Post-16 Network
PRC	Premature retirement compensation
PRE	Pre-retirement education
RCP	Responsive College Programme
SCE	Scottish Certificate of Education
SCOTVEC	Scottish Vocational Education Council
SSR	Student-staff ratio
TA	Training Agency
TC	Training Commission
TCA	Tertiary Colleges Association
TEC	Training and Enterprise Council
TES	Times Educational Supplement
THES	Times Higher Education Supplement
TQM	Total quality management
UK	United Kingdom
US	United States
USP	Unique selling proposition
VET	Vocational education and training
YTS	Youth Training Scheme

Appendix E: References

Audit Commission (1985) **Obtaining better value from further education.** HMSO

Baker, Kenneth (1989) **Further education: a new strategy.** Speech to the Association for Colleges of Further and Higher Education, DES

Bates, Stephen and Meikle, James (1991) Education funds switch to make colleges 'more entrepreneurial', **Guardian**, 22 March p6

Bedfordshire Responsive College Project (1986) **Perceptions of fourth and fifth formers.** Bedfordshire RCP

Bornett, Tim (1990) 'NATFHE as a pressure group', **NATFHE Journal.** Vol 15 No 4 July/August pp33-35

Chesterton, G K (1954) The Invisible Man, in Jepson, R W (ed.) **Short stories by modern writers.** Longmans

Collier, Andrew (1991) A sense of loss, **TES.** 19 April p12

Committee of Directors of Polytechnics (1988) **Services to industry and commerce: technology transfer research, consultancy, training specialist centres and services.** CDP

Cridland, John (1990) All skilled up with somewhere to go: Training and Enterprise Councils, **TES.** 11 May

Crowson, N F and Chapman, M A (1987) **Report on employer perceptions.** Sheffield RCP

Davies, Malcolm (1985) **Politics of pressure: the art of lobbying.** British Broadcasting Corporation

Department of Employment/Department of Education and Science (1984) **Training for jobs** Cm 9135. HMSO

Department of Education and Science *et al* (1989) **Education Statistics for the United Kingdom** 1989 Edition HMSO

Department of Education and Science (1990) International Statistical Comparisons of the Education and Training of 16 to 18 Year Olds. **DES Statistical Bulletin. 1/90 January 1990** HMSO

Department of Education and Science/Department of Employment/Welsh Office (1991) **Education and training for the 21st century**. Cm 1536 Volume I. Cm 1536 Volume II. HMSO

Doherty, G D and Woodhall, E G (1987) **Engineering provision and needs project**. Dudley RCP

Dubs, Alf (1988) **Lobbying, an insider's guide to the parliamentary process**. Pluto

Dunkin, Sean (1987) **School pupils' perceptions of college**. Gwynedd RCP

Education (1991) Labour plans chime with NATFHE. 21 June Vol 177 No 25 p497

Education Management Information Exchange (1989) **Education Management Abstracts**. No 16, December. EMIE

Fonte, Richard and Leach, Ernest R (1986) **Triton College marketing plan, fiscal year 1987**. Triton College

Graystone, John (1991) Essential acronyms in further, higher and adult education. **Mendip Paper MP 011.** The Staff College, Blagdon

Guardian (1990) 11 centres named for voucher-led training. 31 August p4

Guardian (1991) Dead, and buried with much ignominy. (Leading article) 22 March p22

Hall, Vince (1990) **Maintained further education in the United Kingdom**. The Further Education Staff College, Blagdon

Hilton, Barbara (1990) Going further, **Education**. 11 May Vol 175 No 19 p466

Howie, R and Traynor, G (1987) **Employers' perceptions of colleges**. Strathclyde RCP

Independent (1991) A nettle grasped. (Leading article) 22 March p20

Jackson, Mark (1990) Teenagers prepared to stay on - for £3,000, **TES**, 18 May.

Jackson, Mark (1991a) Clarke's emergency stop, **TES**. 29 March.

Jackson, Mark (1991b) Sinking of flagship raises fears for colleges' future, **TES**. 3 May p2

Jones, Idris and Dunkin, Sean (1987) **Employers' perceptions of colleges.** Gwynedd RCP

Lanning, Paula (1990) Message received!, **NATFHE Journal**. Vol 15 No 4 July/August pp11-12

MacLeod, Donald (1991a) Councils lose control of colleges, **Independent**. 22 March p1

MacLeod, Donald (1991b) Truancy figures from schools to be made public, **Independent**. 16 April p5

MacLeod, Donald (1991c) College pays a high price for principal's ambitions, **Independent**. 27 July p3

Maclure, Stuart (1990) Still too many rational drop-outs, **TES**. 25 May

Miller, Charles (1987) **Lobbying government: understanding and influencing the corridors of power**. Blackwell

Morris, Bob (1991) Proceed with caution, **TES**. 22 March

O'Leary, John and Hawkes, Nigel (1990) School standards 'worst in Europe'; Sir Claus Moser. **The Times**. 21 August

Nash, Ian (1991) Clarke's FE plan infuriates Tories, **TES**. 19 April p1

National Foundation for Educational Research (1989) **NFER current projects 1989**. NFER

National Economic Development Office/MSC (1985) **Competence and Competition: Training and Education in the Federal Republic of Germany, the United States and Japan.** NEDO

Pardey, David (1987) **Fifth form survey report**. Suffolk RCP

Spink, David (1988) East Surrey Training Consortium, **Coombe Lodge Report**. Volume 20, Number 9. The Further Education Staff College, Blagdon

TES (1991a) Steal the schools to get out of a poll-tax problem, 22 March

TES (1991b) Freedom balance-sheet for the colleges, 29 March

Theodossin, Ernest (1989a) **Marketing the college**. Blagdon, The Further Education Staff College

Theodossin, Ernest (1989b) **The responsive college**. Blagdon, The Further Education Staff College

Theodossin, Ernest (1989c) **Final report and business plan; feasibility project study for FE Marketing Unit**. The Further Education Staff College, Blagdon [unpublished]

Theodossin, Ernest and Craig Thomson (1987) Developing and Using a Performance Indicator Instrument, **Coombe Lodge Report**. Volume 20, Number 1. The Further Education Staff College, Blagdon

Times (1991) Towards the light, 22 March

Tysome, Tony (1991a) FE leaders fight to keep local links, **THES**. 20 March

Tysome, Tony (1991b) Clarke tackles FE blight, **THES**. 19 April

Tytler, David (1990) The training message decoded, **The Times**. 21 May

Tytler, David (1991) Councils' grip on education loosened, **The Times**, 22 March

Undergraduates of Lancaster University Department of Marketing (1988) **A market research report for the Responsive College Programme**. Lancashire RCP

Willings Press Guide 1990. Reed Information Services (published annually)